bloomsbury
improve your
word power

bloomsbury
improve your
word power

A & C Black • London

3 5 7 9 10 8 6 4

A & C Black Publishers Limited
38 Soho Square
London W1D 3HB
www.acblack.com

© Bloomsbury Publishing Plc 1995, 2002
Additional material © Anna Hodson 1995, 2002

First published 2002 by Bloomsbury Publishing Plc

ISBN 978-0-7136-8531-2

A CIP catalogue record for this book is available from the British Library.

This book is produced using paper that is made from wood grown in
managed, sustainable forests. It is natural, renewable and recyclable.
The logging and manufacturing processes conform to the
environmental regulations of the country of origin.

Typeset by Hewer Text Ltd, Edinburgh

Printed in the UK by Cox & Wyman Ltd, Reading, Berkshire

CONTENTS

INTRODUCTION

DON'T READ THIS BOOK!

Instead, *work* with it. *Write* in it, *talk aloud* to it, *talk back* to it – use your pen or pencil, your voice, not just your eyes and mind.

Learning, *real learning*, goes on only through *active participation*.

When a new word occurs in a chapter, *say it aloud*.

When you do the matching exercise, use a pen or pencil. *Write your responses*.

When you do the 'Yes–No' or 'Same–Opposite' exercises, use your *pen or pencil to indicate the appropriate response*, then check with the key when you have completed the whole exercise.

When you are asked to fill in words that fit definitions, *write your answers*; then check the key both to see if you have responded with the right word and also to make sure your spelling is correct.

When you do the *Review of Etymology* exercises, make sure you fill in the English word containing the prefix, root, or suffix required.

MASTER THE PRONUNCIATION SYSTEM

Saying words *aloud*, and saying them *right*, is half the battle in feeling comfortable and assured with all the new words you are going to learn.

First, master the 'schwa'

Almost every English word of two or more syllables contains one or several syllables in which the vowel sound is said *very* quickly. For example:

'*Linda* spoke to her *mother about* a *different idea* she had.'

Read that aloud. Listen to how the -*a* of *Linda*; the -*er* of *mother*; the *a*- of *about*; the -*ent* of *different*; and the -*a* of *idea* sound.

Very quick – very short! Right?

Phonetically respelt, these words are represented as:

Linda	LIN'-də
mother	MUTH'-ə
about	ə-BOWT'
different	DIF'-rənt
idea	ī-DI'-ə

The symbol 'ə', called a *schwa*, represents the quick, short vowel sound in the five words above.

Next, understand accent

One syllable in every word is stressed, and it is shown in capital letters with an accent mark after it:

railway	RAYL'-way
another	ə-NUTH'-ə

A long word may also have a secondary stress syllable, shown in lower-case letters with an accent mark:

conversational	kon'-vər-SAY'-shən-əl

Both syllables are stressed, but the one in capitals (SAY') sounds stronger or louder than the one in lower-case (kon').

Say all these words aloud, noticing the way the stressed syllables sound.

Consonants

All consonants have their normal sounds, except for *G* (or *g*), which is always pronounced as in *give, get, go*:

agree	ə-GREE'
pagan	PAY'-gən

TH or *th* is pronounced as in *thing*; *T̄H* or *t̄h* is pronounced as in *this*.

ZH or *zh* is pronounced as in *pleasure*.

Be careful of the letter 'S' (or 's') in phonetic respellings. *S* (or *s*) is always *hissed*, as in *see, some, such*. Do not be tempted to *buzz* (or 'voice') the *-s* after final *-ns*:

ambivalence	am-BIV'-ə-ləns

Vowels

The vowel sounds are as follows:

A, a	*cat* (KAT)
E, e	*wet* (WET)
I, i	*sit* (SIT); *ear* (I'-ə); *slowly* (SLŌ'-li)
Ī, ī	*spy* (SPĪ); *civilize* (SIV'-i-līz)
O, o	*knot* (NOT)
U, u	*nut* (NUT)
AH, ah	*car* (KAH); *laughter* (LAHF'-tə)
AW, aw	*for* (FAW); *north* (NAWTH)
AY, ay	*late* (LAYT); *magnate* (MAG'-nayt)
EE, ee	*equal* (EE'-kwəl); *east* (EEST)
ai	*air* (AIR)
əR, ər	*her* (HəR); *earth* (əRTH)
Ō, ō	*toe* (TŌ)
OO, oo	*book* (BOOK); *put* (POOT)
O͞O, o͞o	*doom* (DO͞OM); *muse* (MYO͞OZ)
OOə, ooə	*pure* (PYOOə)
OW, ow	*about* (ə-BOWT')
OY, oy	*soil* (SOYL)
ING, ing	*taking* (TAYK'-ing)

WHY ETYMOLOGY?

Etymology (et'-i-MOL'-ə-ji) deals with the origin or derivation of words.

When you know the meaning of a root (for example, Latin *ego*, I or self), you can better understand, and more easily remember, *all* the words built on this root.

> *Learn one root and you have the key that will unlock the meanings of up to ten or twenty words in which the root appears.*

Learn *ego* and you can immediately get a grasp on *egocentric, egomaniac, egoist, egotist* and *alter ego.*

In the *etymological* (et'-i-mə-LOJ'-i-kəl) approach to vocabulary building:

- You will learn about *prefixes, roots,* and *suffixes*
- You will be able to work out unfamiliar words by recognizing the building blocks from which they are constructed
- You will be able to construct words correctly by learning to put these building blocks together in the proper way.

*Learn how to deal with etymology and you will be able to understand thousands of words you hear or read even if you have never heard or seen these words before.**

WHAT ARE NOUNS, VERBS, AND ADJECTIVES?

You probably know. But if you don't, you can master these parts of speech within the next five minutes.

Nouns

A *noun* is a word that can be preceded directly by *a, an, the, some, such,* or *my:*

An *opportunity* (noun)
Such *heroism* (noun)
The *nation* (noun)

Nouns, you will discover, often end in conventional suffixes: *-ity, -ism, -y, -ion, -ness,* etc.

Verbs

A *verb* is a word describing an action. It fits into the pattern, 'Let us . . .'. A verb has a past tense.

Let us *fraternize* (verb) – past tense: *fraternized*
Let us *magnify* (verb) – past tense: *magnified*

Verbs, you will discover, often end in conventional suffixes: *-ize, -fy, -ate,* etc.

Adjectives

An adjective is a word that fits into the pattern, 'You are very . . .'.

You are very *egoistic* (adjective)
You are very *active* (adjective)

Adjectives, you will discover, often end in conventional suffixes: *-ic, -ed, -ous, -al, -ive,* etc.

Adverbs

These, of course, are generally formed by adding *-ly* to an adjective: *accidental – accidentally; famous – famously,* etc.

That's all there is to it! (Did it take more than five minutes? Maybe ten at the most?)

---

* Incidentally, Latin scholars will notice that I present a Latin verb in the first person singular, present tense (*verto,* I turn), but call it an infinitive (*verto,* to turn).

TEST YOUR PRESENT VOCABULARY

Once – as a child – you were an expert, an accomplished virtuoso, at learning new words. Today, by comparison, you are a rank and bumbling amateur.

Does this statement sound insulting? It may be – but if you are the average adult, it is a statement that is, unfortunately, only too true.

Educational testing indicates that children of ten who have grown up in families in which English is the native language have recognition vocabularies of over twenty thousand words –

And that these same ten-year-olds have been learning new words at a rate of many hundreds a year since the age of four.

In astonishing contrast, studies show that adults who are no longer attending school increase their vocabularies at a pace *slower than twenty-five to fifty words annually.*

How do you assess your own vocabulary?

A test of vocabulary range

Here are thirty brief phrases, each containing one italicized word; it is up to you to find the closest definition of each word. To keep your score valid, refrain from wild guessing. The key will be found at the end of the test.

1. *parry* a blow: (a) ward off, (b) fear, (c) expect, (d) invite, (e) ignore
2. *prevalent* disease: (a) dangerous, (b) catching, (c) childhood, (d) fatal, (e) widespread
3. *ominous* report: (a) loud, (b) threatening, (c) untrue, (d) serious, (e) unpleasant.
4. an *ophthalmologist*: (a) eye doctor, (b) skin doctor, (c) foot doctor, (d) heart doctor, (e) cancer specialist
5. will *supersede* the old law: (a) enforce, (b) specify penalties for, (c) take the place of, (d) repeal, (e) continue
6. an *indefatigable* worker: (a) well-paid, (b) tired, (c) skilful, (d) tireless, (e) pleasant
7. endless *loquacity*: (a) misery, (b) fantasy, (c) repetitiousness, (d) ill health, (e) talkativeness
8. an *incorrigible* optimist: (a) happy, (b) beyond correction or reform, (c) foolish, (d) hopeful, (e) unreasonable
9. a notorious *demagogue*: (a) rabble-rouser, (b) gambler, (c) perpetrator of financial frauds, (d) liar, (e) spendthrift

10. living in *affluence*: (a) difficult circumstances, (b) countrified surroundings, (c) fear, (d) wealth, (e) poverty
11. a *gourmet*: (a) seasoned traveller, (b) greedy eater, (c) vegetarian, (d) connoisseur of good food, (e) skilful chef
12. to *simulate* interest: (a) pretend, (b) feel, (c) lose, (d) stir up, (e) ask for
13. a *magnanimous* action: (a) puzzling, (b) generous, (c) foolish, (d) unnecessary, (e) wise
14. a *clandestine* meeting: (a) prearranged, (b) hurried, (c) important, (d) secret, (e) public
15. to *vacillate* continually: (a) avoid, (b) act indecisively, (c) inject, (d) treat, (e) scold
16. be more *circumspect*: (a) restrained, (b) confident, (c) cautious, (d) honest, (e) intelligent
17. *diaphanous* material: (a) strong, (b) sheer and gauzy, (c) colourful, (d) expensive, (e) synthetic
18. a *taciturn* host: (a) stingy, (b) generous, (c) disinclined to conversation, (d) charming, (e) gloomy
19. to *malign* his friend: (a) accuse, (b) help, (c) disbelieve, (d) slander, (e) introduce
20. a *congenital* deformity: (a) hereditary, (b) crippling, (c) slight, (d) incurable, (e) occurring in the womb or during birth
21. *vicarious* enjoyment: (a) complete, (b) unspoiled, (c) occurring from a feeling of identification with another, (d) long-continuing, (e) temporary
22. *psychogenic* ailment: (a) incurable, (b) contagious, (c) originating in the mind, (d) intestinal, (e) imaginary
23. her *iconoclastic* phase: (a) artistic, (b) sneering at tradition, (c) troubled, (d) difficult, (e) religious
24. a *tyro*: (a) dominating personality, (b) beginner, (c) accomplished musician, (d) dabbler, (e) serious student
25. a *laconic* reply: (a) immediate, (b) assured, (c) terse and meaningful, (d) unintelligible, (e) angry
26. an *anomalous* situation: (a) dangerous, (b) intriguing, (c) unusual, (d) pleasant, (e) unhappy
27. shows *perspicacity*: (a) sincerity, (b) mental keenness, (c) love, (d) faithfulness, (e) longing
28. an unpopular *martinet*: (a) candidate, (b) supervisor, (c) strict disciplinarian, (d) military leader, (e) discourteous snob
29. *gregarious* person: (a) outwardly calm, (b) very sociable, (c) completely untrustworthy, (d) vicious, (e) self-effacing and timid
30. an *inveterate* gambler: (a) impoverished, (b) successful, (c) habitual, (d) occasional, (e) superstitious

Key: 1-a, 2-e, 3-b, 4-a, 5-c, 6-d, 7-e, 8-b, 9-a, 10-d, 11-d, 12-a, 13-b, 14-d, 15-b, 16-c, 17-b, 18-c, 19-d, 20-e, 21-c, 22-c, 23-b, 24-b, 25-c, 26-c, 27-b, 28-c, 29-b, 30-c

Record your score (one point for each correct choice): _____
The meaning of your score:
0–5: below average
6–16: average
17–23: above average
24–27: excellent
28–30: superior

A test of verbal speed

Part 1

In no more than two minutes (time yourself, or have someone time you), decide whether the word in column B is the *same* (or *approximately the same*) in meaning as the word in column A; *opposite* (or *approximately opposite*) in meaning; or whether the two words are merely *different*.

Circle **S** for *same*, **O** for *opposite*, and **D** for *different*.

Column A	Column B			
1. sweet	sour	S	O	D
2. big	angry	S	O	D
3. danger	peril	S	O	D
4. love	hate	S	O	D
5. stand	rise	S	O	D
6. tree	apple	S	O	D
7. doubtful	certain	S	O	D
8. begin	start	S	O	D
9. strange	familiar	S	O	D
10. male	female	S	O	D
11. powerful	weak	S	O	D
12. beyond	under	S	O	D
13. go	get	S	O	D
14. growl	weep	S	O	D
15. open	close	S	O	D
16. chair	table	S	O	D
17. want	desire	S	O	D
18. idle	working	S	O	D
19. rich	luxurious	S	O	D
20. building	structure	S	O	D

Part 2

In no more than three minutes (again, time yourself or have someone time you), write down as many *different* words as you can think of that start with the letter *D*.

Do not use various forms of a word, such as *do, doing, does, done, doer*, etc.

Key: Part 1:   1-O, 2-D, 3-S, 4-O, 5-S, 6-D, 7-O, 8-S, 9-O, 10-O, 11-O, 12-D, 13-D, 14-D, 15-O, 16-D, 17-S, 18-O, 19-S, 20-S

         Part 2:   Any English word starting with *D* is correct unless it is merely another form of a previous word on the list.

Scoring:

Part 1
Score 5 points for each correct answer. Maximum score – 100 points.

Your score on Part 1:   _____

Part 2
Score 1 point for each word.

Your score on Part 2:   _____

Total Score
On Verbal Speed: _____

The meaning of your verbal speed score:

0–50: below average
51–99: average
100–150: above average
151–200: excellent

A test of verbal responsiveness

Part 1

Write in the blank in column B a word starting with the letter *P* that is the <u>same</u>, or *approximately the same*, in meaning as the word given in column A:

    Example: look   *peer*

    Remember: Every answer *must* start with the letter *P*.

A   B
1. bucket   _____
2. faultless   _____
3. maybe   _____
4. forgive   _____
5. separate   _____
6. likely   _____
7. annoy   _____
8. good-looking _____
9. picture   _____
10. choose   _____

Part 2

Write in the blank in column B a word starting with the letter *G* that is *opposite, approximately opposite*, or *in contrast to* the word given in column A.

    Example: stop   *go*

    Remember: Every answer *must* start with the letter *G*.

A   B
1. lose   _____
2. midget   _____
3. special   _____
4. lady   _____
5. take   _____
6. moron   _____
7. sad   _____
8. boy   _____
9. happy   _____
10. awkward   _____

Key: Part 1:   Where more than one answer is given below, count as correct any word you have written that is the same as any *one* of the answers.

1-pail, 2-perfect, 3-perhaps, possibly, probably, 4-pardon, 5-part, 6-probable, possible, perhaps, 7-pester, 8-pretty, 9-photograph, painting, 10-pick

Part 2: Where more than one answer is given below, count as correct any word you have written that is the same as any *one* of the answers.

1-gain, get, garner, grab, glean, grasp, grip, 2-giant, gigantic, great, gross, 3-general, 4-gentleman, 5-give, 6-genius, 7-glad, gleeful, gleesome, 8-girl, 9-gloomy, glum, grieving, grumpy, 10-graceful

Scoring:

Score Parts 1 and 2 together. Write in the blank the *total number of correct responses you gave*: _____

The meaning of your verbal responsiveness score:

0–5: below average
6–10: average
11–15: above average
16–18: excellent
19–20: superior

Vocabulary and success

Now you know where you stand. If you are in the below average or average groups, you must consider, seriously, whether an inadequate vocabulary may be holding you back. If you scored above average, excellent, or superior, you have doubtless already discovered the unique and far-reaching value of a rich vocabulary, and you are eager to add still further to your knowledge of words.

You can increase your vocabulary

The more extensive your vocabulary, the better your chances of success, other things being equal – success in attaining your educational goals, success in moving ahead in your business or professional career, success in achieving your intellectual potential.

And you *can* increase your vocabulary – faster and more easily than you may realize.

HOW TO WORK FOR BEST RESULTS

If you intend to work with this book seriously, that is, if your clear intention is to add a thousand or more new words to your present vocabulary – add them permanently, unforgettably, add them so successfully that you will soon find yourself using them in speech and writing – I suggest that you give yourself every advantage by carefully following the laws of learning:

Space your learning

Every chapter will be divided into 'sessions'. Each session may take half an hour to an hour and a half, depending on the amount of material and on your own speed of learning.

Do one or two sessions at a time – three if you're going strong and are very involved – and always decide when you stop *exactly when* you will return.

Do not rush – go at your own comfortable speed

Everyone learns at a different pace. Fast learners are no better than slow learners – it's the end result that counts, not the time it takes you to finish.

Review

When you start a new session, go back to the last exercise of the previous session, cover your answers, and test your retention – do you have quick recall after a day or so has elapsed?

Test yourself

You are not aiming for a grade, or putting your worth on the line, when you take the Tests – rather you are discovering your weaknesses, if any; deciding where repairs have to be made; and, especially, experiencing a feeling of success at work well done. (In learning, too, nothing succeeds like success!)

But most important – develop a routine and stick to it!

Places into names

Very many things are called after the place where they were invented, or where they were made.

manila – the brown paper used for making envelopes is called after *Manila*, the capital of the Philippines, where the hemp that it is made from is grown.

denim – the original full name was *serge de Nîmes*, meaning serge (strong diagonally woven cloth) from *Nîmes*, in France. From *de Nîmes* we get denim.

ermine – the white winter coat of the stoat, made into robes for lords and judges, is named after *Armenia*, where it is supposed to come from.

limousine – the posh kind of motor car is named from the type of cloak with a hood worn by the peasants of the province of *Limousin*, in central France.

bantam – the miniature hen is called after *Bantam*, a village in Java in the East Indies.

damask – the beautiful fabric with flowers or arabesque patterns woven in is called after *Damascus*, capital of Syria. The same place has also given its name to the *damson*, a dark-red plum.

CHAPTER 1
WORDS FOR ACTIONS

Verbs are incalculably useful to you. Every sentence you think, say, read, or write contains an implied or expressed verb, for it is the verb that carries the action, the movement, the force of your ideas.

The richer and more extensive your vocabulary of verbs, the more accurately and expressively you can communicate your understanding of actions, reactions, attitudes, and emotions.

SESSION 1 – VERBS TO GET YOU OFF THE GROUND

1. Playing it down

Jim has won the school tennis tournament. But Sally says that if Jack hadn't been sidelined with a broken ankle, he would have won; Jim isn't really the best.

What is Sally doing?

She is *disparaging* Jim's achievement.

2. Playing it safe

Plans are published for a by-pass round your town. Business people are appalled, because they say it will ruin their trade. Old people and parents of young children are pleased, because the roads will be safer for them. What does your MP say? He says the by-pass is good in some ways, bad in others.

For it or against it?

Your MP is *equivocating*.

3. Enjoying the little things

Have you ever seen a play or film that was so charming that you felt sheer delight as you watched? Or perhaps you have had a portion of lemon meringue pie that was the last word in gustatory enjoyment?

How do such things affect you?

They *titillate* you.

4. Hero worship

You know how teenagers of an earlier generation idolized the Beatles, the Rolling Stones, Rod Stewart?

And of course you know how certain people fall all over visiting celebrities – they show them ingratiating attention and flatter them fulsomely.

Emphasize

They *adulate* such celebrities.

5. Accentuating the negative

The big match is next week, and the team must train hard. The manager tells the players: 'No alcohol, no chocolate, no binges.'

What, in one word, is the manager doing?

He is *proscribing* harmful items in their diet.

6. Accentuating the affirmative

You are warm, enthusiastic, outgoing, easy to please; you are quick to show appreciation, yet accept the human weaknesses of others.

You are a fascinating talker, an even better listener.

Need you have any fears about making friends? Obviously not.

Your characteristics *obviate* such fears.

7. Playing it wrong

What about neurotic people who unconsciously wish to fail? In business interviews they say exactly the wrong words, they do exactly the wrong things, they seem intent (as, *unconsciously*, they actually are) on ensuring failure, though consciously they are doing their best to succeed.

What effect does such a neurotic tendency have?

It *militates* against success.

8. Playing it dirty

'Steve? *He's a closet alcoholic.* Emma? *She's sleeping around* – and her stupid husband doesn't suspect a thing. Bill? *He's embezzling from his own company.* Paul? *He's a child molester.*'

What is this character doing?

He's *maligning* everyone.

9. Giving the benefit of any doubt

Do you think it's all right to cheat on your income tax? At least just a little? Doesn't everybody do it?

How do you feel about marital infidelity? Are you inclined to overlook the occasional 'bit on the side'?

If your answers are in the affirmative, how are you reacting to such legal or ethical transgressions?

You *condone* them.

10. Changing hostility

Unwittingly you have done something that has aroused anger in your best friend, and he makes it obvious that he feels bitter. His friendship is valuable to you and you wish to restore yourself in his good graces. What do you do?

You try to *placate* him.

Can you match the words in the first column with those in the second?

1. disparage   a. flatter lavishly
2. equivocate   b. work against
3. titillate   c. prohibit
4. adulate   d. forgive
5. proscribe·   e. change hostility to friendliness
6. obviate   f. purposely talk in such a way as to be vague and misleading
7. militate·   g. slander
8. malign   h. play down
9. condone·   i. make unnecessary
10. placate   j. tickle; stimulate pleasurably

Key: 1-h, 2-f, 3-j, 4-a, 5-c, 6-i, 7-b, 8-g, 9-d, 10-e

Do you understand the words?

1. Do you normally *disparage* something you admire?   YES NO
2. Do you *equivocate* if you think it unwise to take a definite stand?   YES NO
3. Do pleasant things *titillate* you?   YES NO
4. Do emotionally mature people need constant *adulation*?   YES NO
5. Is sugar *proscribed* for most diabetics?   YES NO
6. Does a substantial fortune *obviate* financial fears?   YES NO
7. Does a worker's inefficiency often *militate* against his keeping his job?   YES NO
8. Do people enjoy being *maligned*?   YES NO
9. Do we generally *condone* the faults of those we love?   YES NO
10. Can you sometimes *placate* a person by apologizing?   YES NO

Key: 1-N, 2-Y, 3-Y, 4-N, 5-Y, 6-Y, 7-Y, 8-N, 9-Y, 10-Y

SESSION 2 – SOME WORDS ARE MORE EQUAL THAN OTHERS

1. Equality

If you play golf, you know that each course or hole has a certain *par*, the number of strokes allowed according to the results achieved by expert players. Your own accomplishment on the course will be at *par*, above *par*, or below *par*.

Par is from a Latin word meaning *equal*. You may try, when you play golf, to *equal* the expert score; and some days you may, or may not, feel *equal* to your usual self.

So when you *disparage* (dis-PAR'-ij), you lower someone's *par*, or feeling of *equality* (*dis-* may be a negative prefix). The noun is *disparagement* (dis-PAR'-ij-mənt), the adjective *disparaging* (dis-PAR'-ij-ing), as in 'Why do you always make *disparaging* remarks about me?'

Parity (PAR'-i-ti) as a noun means *equality*; *disparity* (dis-PAR'-ə-tee) means a lack of *equality*, or a difference. The adjective *disparate* (DIS'-pə-rət) indicates *essential* or *complete difference* or *inequality*, as in 'Our philosophies are so *disparate* that we can never come to any agreement on action.'

The word *compare* and all its forms (*comparable, comparative*, etc.) derive from *par*, equal. Two things are *compared* when they have certain *equal* or similar qualities (*con-, com-*, together, with).

Pair and *peer* are also from *par*. Things (shoes, socks, gloves, etc.) in *pairs* are *equal*; your *peers* are those *equal* to you, as in age, rank, or ability.

2. How to say yes and no

Equivocate is built on another Latin word meaning *equal* – *aequus* (the spelling in English is always *equ-*) – plus *vox, vocis*, voice.

When you *equivocate* (i-KWIV'-ə-kayt'), you seem to be saying both *yes* and *no* with *equal voice*. An *equivocal* (i-KWIV'-ə-kəl) answer is deliberately vague and susceptible of contradictory interpretations, quite the opposite of an *unequivocal* (un'-i-KWIV'-ə-kəl) response, which says *Yes!* or *No!* Politicians are masters of *equivocation* (i-kwiv'-ə-KAY'-shən) – on most vital issues they sit on the fence.

3. Statements of various kinds

Do not confuse *equivocal* with *ambiguous* (am-BIG'yoo-əs). An *equivocal* statement is purposely (and with malice aforethought) couched in language that will be deceptive; an *ambiguous* statement can have two possible interpretations, either deliberately or accidentally, but without malicious intent.

Ambi is a root meaning *both*; anything *ambiguous* may have *both* one meaning and another meaning. If you say 'That sentence is the height of *ambiguity*', you mean that you find it vague because it may mean two different things. *Ambiguity* is pronounced am'-bi-GYŌO-i-ti.

Another type of statement or word contains the possibility of two interpretations – one of them suggestive or sexy. Such a statement or word is a *double entendre*. This is from the French and translates literally as *double meaning*. Give the word as close a French pronunciation as you can – DOOB'-lahn-TAHN'-drə.

Review of etymology

Write in the space provided an English word that uses each prefix, root or suffix.

1. *par*	equal		PARITY
2. *-ment*	noun suffix attached to verbs		disparagement
3. *-ity*	noun suffix attached to adjectives		equity / parity ambiguity
4. *dis-*	negative prefix		disparaging /dis pursu
5. *con-, com-*	with, together		compare / com
6. *aequus (equ-)*	equal		equivocal
7. *vox, vocis*	voice		
8. *-ate*	verb suffix		
9. *-ous*	adjective suffix		ambiguous
10. *ambi-*	both		ambivalent

Can you match the words?

1. parity		a.	belittlement
2. disparity		b.	act of being deliberately vague or indirectly deceptive
3. disparagement		c.	quality of being open to misinterpretation
4. peer		d.	statement or word with two meanings, one of them risqué
5. equivocation		e.	inequality
6. ambiguity		f.	equality
7. double entendre		g.	one's equal
8. unequivocal		h.	completely different
9. par		i.	definitely positive or negative
10. disparate		j.	equal

Key: 1-f, 2-e, 3-a, 4-g, 5-b, 6-c, 7-d, 8-i, 9-j, 10-h

Do you understand the words?

1. Is there a *disparity* in age between a
   grandfather and his granddaughter?   YES   NO
2. Is an *equivocal* statement clear and direct?   YES   NO
3. Is an *unequivocal* answer vague and misleading?   YES   NO
4. Are politicians often masters of *equivocation*?   YES   NO
5. Are *ambiguous* sentences somewhat confusing?   YES   NO
6. Are people with *disparate* perceptions of life
   likely to experience reality in the same way?   YES   NO
7. Is a *disparaging* look one of admiration?   YES   NO
8. When people *equivocate*, are they evading the issue? YES   NO
9. Is the deliberate use of *double entendres* likely to
   shock puritanical people?   YES   NO
10. Are supervisors and their subordinates *peers*?   YES   NO

Key: 1-Y, 2-N, 3-N, 4-Y, 5-Y, 6-N, 7-N, 8-Y, 9-Y, 10-N

SESSION 3 – HORSES FOR COURSES

1. More on equality

The root *aequus*, spelled *equ-* in English words, is a building block of:
1. *equity* (EK'-wi-ti) – justice, fairness; i.e., equal treatment. Stocks
in the financial markets are *equities*, and the value of your home over
and above the amount of the mortgage you owe is your *equity* in it. The
adjective is *equitable* (EK'-wi-tə-bəl).
2. *inequity* (in-EK'-wi-ti) – injustice, unfairness (*equity* plus the
negative prefix *in-*). Adjective: *inequitable* (in-EK'-wi-tə-bəl).
3. *iniquity* (in-IK'-wi-ti) – the change of a single letter (*e* to *i*)
extends the meaning of a word far beyond its derivation. Injustice and
unfairness are sinful and wicked, so an *iniquity* is a sin or vice, and
iniquity is wickedness, sinfulness. Adjective: *iniquitous* (in-IK'-wi-təs).
4. *equinox* (EE'-kwi-noks' *or* EK'-wi-noks') – 'equal night', a
combination of *aequus* and *nox, noctis*, night. The *equinox*, when
day and night are of equal length, occurs twice a year, on 21 March
and 21 September. The adjective is *equinoctial* – ee-'kwi-NOK'-shəl
or ek'-wi-NOK'-shəl. *Nocturnal* (nok-TURN'-əl), derived from
nox, noctis, describes people, animals, or plants that are active or
flourish at night rather than during daylight hours. A *nocturne*
(NOK'-turn) is a musical composition of dreamy character (i.e.,
night music), or a painting of a night scene.

5. *equanimity* (ee-'kwə-NIM'-i-ti *or* ek'-wə–NIM'-ti) – etymologically *aequus* plus *animus*, mind, hence 'equal mind'. You will be admired if you can maintain your *equanimity* when everyone around you is getting excited or upset.

6. *equability* (ek'-wə-BIL'-i-ti) – a close synonym of *equanimity*. A person of *equable* (EK'-wə-bəl) temperament is characteristically calm, serene, unflappable, even-tempered.

7. *equilibrium* (ee'-kwi-LIB'-ri-əm *or* ek'-wi-LIB'-ri-əm) – by derivation *aequus* plus *libra*, balance, weight, pound, hence 'equal balance'. *Libra* (LĪ'-brə) is the seventh sign of the zodiac, represented by a pair of scales. (That is why the abbreviation for the word *pound*, a weight, is *lb* and the symbol for *pound*, the monetary unit, is £.) *Equilibrium* is a state of physical balance, especially between opposing forces. When you are very drunk you may have difficulty keeping your *equilibrium*.

The *equator* divides the earth into *equal* halves, and words like *equation*, *equivalent*, *equidistant*, *equiangular*, and *equilateral* (from Latin *latus*, *lateris*, side) are self-explanatory.

2. Not to be confused with horses

Equestrian (i-KWES'-tri-ən) is someone on a horse (as *pedestrian* is someone on foot); an *equestrienne* (i-kwes'-tri-əN') is a woman on a horse (if you *must* make the distinction); and *equine* (E'-kwīn) is like a horse, as in appearance or characteristics, or descriptive of horses.

Equestrian is also an adjective referring to horseback riding, as an *equestrian* statue; and *equine* is also a noun, i.e., a horse.

So the *equ-* in these words, from Latin *equus*, horse, is not to be confused with the *equ-* in the words of the previous section which is from *aequus*, equal.

3. Do you hear voices?

Equivocal, you should recall, combines *aequus* with *vox, vocis*, voice; and *vox, vocis* combines with *fero*, to bear or carry, to form *vociferous* (vō-SIF'-ər-əs), 'carrying (much) voice', hence loud, noisy, clamorous, as *vociferous* demands (not at all quiet or subtle).

If you are *vocal* (VŌ'-kəl), you express yourself readily and freely by voice: *vocal* music is sung, and you know what your *vocal* cords are for.

To *vocalize* (VŌ'-kə-līz') is to give voice to ('*vocalize* your anger, don't hold it in!'), or to sing the *vocals* (or voice parts) of music. (Can you write the noun form of the verb *vocalize*? _____)
A *vocalist* (VŌ'-kə-list) is a singer.

Review of etymology

Write in the space provided an English word that uses each prefix, root, or suffix.

1. *aequus (equ-)*   equal   _____
2. *in-*   negative prefix   _____
3. *nox, noctis*   night   _____
4. *animus*   mind   _____
5. *libra*   balance, weight, pound   _____
6. *-ist*   person who   _____
7. *latus, lateris*   side   _____
8. *equus*   horse   _____
9. *vox, vocis*   voice   _____
10. *fero*   to bear, carry   _____

Can you match the words?

1. equity   a. time when night and day are of equal
                      length
2. inequity   b. balance of mind; composure
3. iniquity   c. horseback rider
4. equinox   d. a horse
5. nocturne   e. sinfulness; wickedness
6. equanimity   f. unfairness, injustice
7. equilibrium   g. noisy, clamorous
8. equestrian   h. night music
9. vociferous   i. fairness, justice
10. equine   j. balance

Key: 1-i, 2-f, 3-e, 4-a, 5-h, 6-b, 7-j, 8-c, 9-g, 10-d

Do you understand the words?

1. Is life always *equitable*?   YES NO
2. Does the cynic expect more *inequity* than *equity*
   in life?   YES NO
3. Do ethical people practice *iniquity*?   YES NO
4. Does the *equinox* occur once a month?   YES NO
5. Are *nocturnal* animals active at night?   YES NO
6. If you preserve your *equanimity*, do you often get
   excited?   YES NO
7. Is it easy to maintain your *equilibrium* on icy
   ground?   YES NO

8. Is *equability* the mark of a calm, even-tempered person?   YES NO
9. Does an *equilateral* triangle have equal sides?   YES NO
10. Is an *equine* a dog?   YES NO

Key: 1-N, 2-Y, 3-N, 4-N, 5-Y, 6-N, 7-N, 8-Y, 9-Y, 10-N

SESSION 4 – THE FEEL-GOOD FACTOR

1. How to tickle

Titillate comes from a Latin verb meaning *to tickle*. You can (figuratively) *titillate* people, or their minds, fancies, or palates by charm, brilliance, wit, promises, or in many other ways.

Titillation (tit'-i-LAY'-shən) has the added meaning of light sexual stimulation.

2. How to flatter

A *compliment* is a courteous expression of praise; *flattery* is stronger, and often insincere. *Adulation* (ad'-yoo-LAY'-shən) is flattery and worship carried to an excessive degree. (The derivation is from a Latin verb meaning *to fawn upon*.) The adjective is *adulatory* (ad'-yoo-LAY'-tə-ri).

3. Ways of writing

Proscribe, to forbid, is commonly used for medical, religious, or legal prohibitions. For example, the church *proscribes*, or announces a *proscription* (prō-SKRIP'-shən) against, such activities as may harm its parishioners. The derivation is the prefix *pro-*, before, plus *scribo, scriptus*, to write.

Scribo, scriptus is the building block of scores of common English words: *scribe, scribble, prescribe, describe, subscribe, script, the Scriptures, manuscript, typescript*, etc. *Describe* uses the prefix *de-*, down – to *describe* is, etymologically, 'to write down' about. *Manuscript*, combining *manus*, hand (as in *manual* labour), with *scriptus*, is something handwritten. The *Scriptures* are holy writings. To *subscribe* (as to a magazine) is to write one's name *under* an order or contract (*sub*, under, as in *subway, subsurface*, etc.). To *inscribe* is to write *in* or *into* (a book, for example, or metal or stone). A *postscript* is something written after (Latin *post*, after) the main part is finished.

Note how -*scribe* verbs change to nouns and adjectives:

    describe   description   descriptive

4. It's obvious

You are familiar with the word *via*, by way of, which is from the Latin word for *road*. When something is *obvious*, etymologically it is right there in the middle of the road where no one can fail to see it. And if you meet an obstacle in the road and dispose of it forthwith, you are doing what *obviate* (OB'-vi-ayt) says. Thus, if you review your work daily in some college subject, frenzied 'cramming' at the end of the term will be *obviated*. The noun is *obviation* (ob'-vi-AY'-shən).

5. War

Militate (MIL'-i-tayt) derives from *militis*, one of the forms of the Latin noun meaning *soldier* or *fighting man*. If something *militates* against you, it fights against you, i.e., works to your disadvantage.

The adjective *militant* (MIL'-i-tənt) comes from the same root. The noun is *militancy* (MIL'-i-tən-si), and *militant* is also a noun for the person – 'Steve is a *militant* in the Animal Liberation movement'.

6. First the bad news

Built on Latin *malus*, bad, evil, to *malign* (mə-LĪN) is to speak evil about, to defame, to slander. *Malign* is also an adjective meaning bad, harmful, evil, hateful. Another adjective form is *malignant* (mə-LIG'-nənt), as in 'a *malignant* glance' or 'a *malignant* growth', i.e., one that is cancerous (bad).

The noun of *malignant* is *malignancy* (mə-LIG'-nən-si), which, medically, is a cancerous growth, or, generally, the condition of harmfulness. The noun form of the adjective *malign* is *malignity* (mə-LIG'-nə-ti).

Observe how we can construct English words by combining *malus* with other Latin roots.

Add the root *dico, dictus*, to say or tell, to form *malediction* (mal'-ə-DIK'-shən), a curse, i.e., an evil saying. Adjective: *maledictory* (mal'-ə-DIK'-tə-ri).

Add the root *volo*, to wish, to will, or to be willing, and we can construct the adjective *malevolent* (mə-LEV'-ə-lent), wishing evil or harm – a *malevolent* glance, attitude, feeling, etc. The noun is *malevolence* (mə-LEV'-ə-ləns).

Add the root *facio, factus*, to do or make (also spelled, in English words, *fec-, fic-, factus*, or, as a verb ending, *fy*), to form *malefactor* (MAL'-i-fak'-tə) – a wrongdoer, a criminal – a *malefactor* commits a *malefaction* (mal'-i-FAK'-shən), an evil deed.

Other common words also spring from Latin *malus*: words like *maladjusted, malcontent, malpractice, malnutrition*, etc., all with the connotation of *badness*.

Review of etymology

Write in the space provided an English word that uses each prefix,
root, or suffix.

1. *scribo, scriptus*	to write	_____
2. *manus*	hand	_____
3. *sub-*	under	_____
4. *via*	road	_____
5. *militis*	soldier	_____
6. *malus*	bad, evil	_____
7. *dico, dictus*	to say, tell	_____
8. *volo*	to wish	_____
9. *facio (fec-, fic-, -fy)*	to do, make	_____
10. *-ence, -ancy*	noun suffix	_____

Can you match the words?

1. titillation	a. prohibition
2. adulation	b. hatefulness; harmfulness
3. proscription	c. clumsiness
4. militancy	d. quality of wishing evil; ill-will
5. malignity	e. fact or act of making unnecessary or of doing away with
6. malediction	f. worship; excessive flattery
7. maladroitness	g. a wrongdoer
8. obviation	h. pleasurable stimulation; tickling
9. malevolence	i. a curse
10. malefactor	j. aggressiveness

Key: 1-h, 2-f, 3-a, 4-j, 5-b, 6-i, 7-c, 8-e, 9-d, 10-g

Do you understand the words?

1. Does a *malignant* look indicate kindly feelings?	YES	NO
2. Is a cancer sometimes called a *malignancy*?	YES	NO
3. Is a *manuscript* written with a typewriter?	YES	NO
4. If the play is a tragedy, do you expect to be *titillated* by it?	YES	NO
5. Do people enjoy having *maledictions* hurled at them?	YES	NO
6. Is a *maleficent* act likely to cause harm or hurt?	YES	NO
7. Does *maladroitness* show skill?	YES	NO

8. Is a *malefactor* a good person?   YES NO
9. Does an *adulatory* attitude show exaggerated
   admiration?   YES NO
10. Is *militancy* the same as passiveness?   YES NO

Key: 1-N, 2-Y, 3-N, 4-N, 5-N, 6-Y, 7-N, 8-N, 9-Y, 10-N

SESSION 5 – GOOD AND BAD IN EVERYONE

1. So now what's the good news?

Malus is *bad*; *bonus is good*. The adverb from the Latin adjective *bonus*
is *bene*, and *bene* is the root found in words that contrast with the
mal- terms we studied in the previous session.

So *benign* (bi-NIN') and *benignant* (bi-NIG'-nənt) are kindly, not
harmful, as in a *benign* judge, a *benign* tumour (not cancerous), a
benignant attitude to wrongdoers. The corresponding nouns are
benignity (bi-NIG'-ni-ti) and *benignancy* (bi-NIG'-nən-si).

A *malediction* is a curse; a *benediction* (ben'-i-DIK'-shən) is a bles-
sing, a 'saying good'. The adjective is *benedictory* (ben'-i-DIK'-tə-ri).

In contrast to *maleficent* is *beneficent* (bi-NEF'-i-sənt), doing good.
The noun is *beneficence* (bi-NEF'-i-səns).

In contrast to *malefactor* is *benefactor* (BEN'-i-fak'-tə), one who
does good things for another; a woman who does this is a *benefac-
tress* (BEN'-i-fak'-tris). And the person receiving the *benefaction*
(ben-i-FAK'-shən) is a *beneficiary* (ben'-i-FISH'-ər-i).

So let others be *malevolent* towards you – confuse them by being
benevolent (bi-NEV'-ə-lənt) – wish them well.

The adjective *bonus*, good, is found in English *bonus*, extra payment,
and in *bona fide* (BŌ-nə-FĪ-di), etymologically, 'in good faith', hence
valid, without pretence – as a *bona fide* offer. *Fides* is Latin for *faith* or *trust*,
as in *fidelity* (fi-DEL'-i-ti), faithfulness, and *infidelity* (in'-fi-DEL'-i-ti)
(Latin *in-*, not), unfaithfulness, especially to the marriage vows.

2. Saying, doing, wishing

Dictate, dictator, dictation, dictatorial (dik'-tə-TAWR'-i-əl) – words
that signify telling others what to do – are built on *dico, dictus*, to say, as
is *predict*, to tell beforehand (*pre-*, before).

Contradict, to say against, or to make an opposite statement, combines *dico* with *contra-*, against, opposite; and *addiction*, etymologically
'a saying to or towards', combines *dico* with *ad-*, to, towards.

Facio, factus means to do or make. Thus *factory* is a place where things are *made* (*-ory*, place where); *fiction*, something *made* up or invented; *artificial*, *made* by human art rather than occurring in nature; and *clarify*, *simplify*, and *magnify* (*magnus*, large) among hundreds of other *-fy* verbs.

Volo, to wish, to be willing (as in *malevolent*, *benevolent*), occurs in *voluntary*, *involuntary*, *volunteer*, each expressing *wish* or *willingness*. Less common, and from the same root, is *volition* (və-LISH'-ən), the act or power of willing or wishing, as in 'of her own volition'.

Teaser questions for the amateur etymologist – 1

1. Thinking of the roots *animus* (mind) in *equanimity* and *magnus* (large) in *magnify*, can you combine these two roots to form a noun meaning, etymologically, *largeness of mind*? Can you work out the adjectival form, ending in *-ous*, of the noun you have constructed?

2. If *equilateral* means *equal-sided*, can you construct an adjective meaning *two-sided*?

3. *Trans-* is a prefix meaning *across*. Build a verb meaning *to write across* (from one form or language to another). What is the noun derived from this verb?

4. What disease was so named on the erroneous assumption that it was caused by 'bad air'?

5. *Facio* (to make) may appear in English words as *fec-*. Using the prefix *con-*, together, can you form a noun sometimes used as a synonym for a sweet, cake, or ice cream (etymologically, 'something made together')?

(*Answers in Chapter 11*)

---

3. If you please!

Placate is built on the root *plac-* which derives from two related Latin verbs meaning (1) *to please* and (2) *to appease* or *pacify*.

If you succeed in *placating* an angry colleague, you turn that person's hostile attitude into one that is friendly or favourable. The noun is *placation* (plə-KAY'-shən), the adjective either *placative* (plə-KAY'-tiv *or* PLAK'-ə-tiv) *or* *placatory* (plə-KAY'-tə-ri *or* PLAK'-ə-tə-ri). A person who can be soothed, whose hostility can be changed to friendliness, is *placable* (PLAK'-ə-bəl). The opposite is *implacable* (im-PLAK'-ə-bəl), which has taken on the added meaning of *unyielding to entreaty or pity*; hence, *harsh, relentless*.

The noun form of *implacable* is *implacability* (im-plak'-ə-BIL'-i-ti). Can you say the noun derived from *placable*?

If you are *placid* (PLAS'-id), you are calm, easygoing, undisturbed – etymologically, you are pleased with things as they are. The noun is *placidity* (plə-SID'-i-ti).

If you are *complacent* (kəm-PLAY'-sənt), you are pleased with yourself (*com-*, from *con-*, with, together); you may, in fact, be *too* pleased with yourself for your own good. The noun is *complacence* (kəm-PLAY'-səns) or *complacency* (kəm-PLAY'sən-si).

4. How to give – and forgive

To *condone* (kon-DŌN') is to forgive or be uncritical of (an offence or an antisocial act). You may *condone* shoplifting from a supermarket or exceeding the speed limit, though you personally observe the law with scrupulousness. The noun is *condonation* (kon'-dō-NAY'-shən).

Condone is built on Latin *dono*, to give, the root found in *donor*, one who gives; *donate*, to give; and *donation*, a gift.

Review of etymology

Write in the space provided an English word that uses each prefix, root, or suffix.

1. *bonus, bene*	good, well	_____
2. *fides*	faith	_____
3. *dico, dictus*	to say, tell	_____
4. *pre-*	before, beforehand	_____
5. *contra*	against, opposite	_____
6. *facio, factus, fec-, fic-, -fy*	to make or do	_____
7. *manus*	hand	_____
8. *volo*	to wish, to will, to be willing	_____
9. *plac-*	to please, appease, soothe, pacify	_____
10. *dono*	to give	_____

Can you match the words?

1. benign
2. benedictory
3. volition
4. bona fide
5. dictatorial
6. placatory
7. implacable
8. placid
9. complacent
10. fidelity

a. free will
b. domineering; giving orders in a manner permitting no refusal
c. not to be soothed or pacified; unyielding to pity or entreaty
d. tending to pacify or to change hostility to friendliness
e. kindly, good-natured, not cancerous
f. faithfulness
g. self-satisfied; smug
h. of the nature of, or relating to, blessings
i. in good faith; sincere; valid
j. calm, unruffled, undisturbed

Key: 1-e, 2-h, 3-a, 4-i, 5-b, 6-d, 7-c, 8-j, 9-g, 10-f

Do you understand the words?

1. Are *benedictions* given in houses of worship? YES NO
2. Is it pleasant to be the recipient of a *beneficent* act? YES NO
3. Are kind people *benevolent*? YES NO
4. Do *placatory* gestures often heal wounds and soothe disgruntled friends? YES NO
5. Are some unambitious people *complacent*? YES NO
6. Does *benignity* show malice? YES NO
7. Is a *benefaction* an act of philanthropy? YES NO
8. Is an *implacable* foe of corruption likely to *condone* corrupt acts? YES NO
9. Is a *bona fide* offer made insincerely? YES NO
10. Does a *benignant* attitude indicate hostility? YES NO

Key: 1-Y, 2-Y, 3-Y, 4-Y, 5-Y, 6-N, 7-Y, 8-N, 9-N, 10-N

Worldwide words

Can you guess which languages (or where in the world) these words come from?

1. *budgerigar*
2. *robot*
3. *anorak*
4. *beserk*
5. *mammoth*

6. *bangle*
7. *chocolate*
8. *ombudsman*
9. *ukulele*
10. *safari*

Answers: 1-an Australian Aboriginal language, 2-Czech, 3-Inuit (Eskimo), 4-Icelandic, 5-Russian, 6-Hindi (India), 7-Aztec (Central America), 8-Swedish, 9-Hawaiian, 10-Swahili (East Africa)

CHAPTER 2
SPEECH AND SILENCE

Perhaps some of your richest and most satisfying experiences have been with people to whom you can just talk, talk, talk. As you speak, previously untapped springs of ideas and emotions begin to flow; you hear yourself saying things you never thought you knew.

In this chapter we look at ten types of people you might be talking to, discovering the adjective that aptly describes each one.

SESSION 6 – THE STRONG, SILENT TYPE?

1. Saying little

There are some people who just don't like to talk. It's not that they prefer to listen. For these people conversation is a bore, even a painful waste of time. Try to engage them, and the best you may expect for your efforts is a noncommittal grunt or an impatient silence. Finally you give up, thinking 'Are they self-conscious? Do they hate people? Do they hate *me*?'.

The adjective: *taciturn*

2. Saying little – meaning much

There is an anecdote about Calvin Coolidge, who was president of the USA in the 1920s. A young newspaperwoman was sitting next to him at a banquet, so the story goes, and turned to him mischievously.

'Mr Coolidge,' she said. 'I have a bet with my editor that I can get you to say more than two words to me this evening.'

'*You lose*,' replied Coolidge.

The adjective: *laconic*

3. When the words won't come

Under the pressure of some strong emotion – fear, rage, or anger – people may find it almost impossible to get their feelings untangled enough to form understandable sentences. They undoubtedly have a lot they want to say, but the best they can do is splutter!

    The adjective: *inarticulate*

4. Much talk, little sense

Miss Bates, a character in the novel *Emma*, by Jane Austen, says:

    'So obliging of you! No, we should not have heard, if it had not been for this particular circumstance, of her being able to come here so soon. My mother is so delighted. For she is to be three months with us at least. Three months, she says so, positively, as I am going to have the pleasure of reading to you. The case is, you see, that the Campbells are going to Ireland. Mrs Dixon has persuaded her father and mother to come over and see her directly. I was going to say, but, however, different countries, and so she wrote a very urgent letter to her mother, or her father, I declare I do not know which it was, but we shall see presently in Jane's letter . . .'

    The adjective: *garrulous*

5. Unoriginal

Some people are completely lacking in originality and imagination – and their talk shows it. Their words abound in clichés and stereotypes, their phraseology is without sparkle.

    The adjective: *banal*

6. Words, words, words!

They talk and talk and talk, never using one word where ten would do instead. They phrase, rephrase, and re-rephrase their thoughts, clothing them in long and important-sounding words.

    The adjective: *verbose*

7. Words in quick succession

They are rapid, fluent talkers, the words seeming to roll off their tongues with such ease and lack of effort that you listen with amazement.

    The adjective: *voluble*

8. Words that convince

They express their ideas clearly and persuasively, and in a way that calls for wholehearted agreement from an intelligent listener.

The adjective: *cogent*

9. The sound and the fury

Their talk is noisy and vehement. What may be lacking in content is compensated for in force and loudness.

The adjective: *vociferous*

10. Quantity

They talk a great deal – a very great deal. They may be voluble, vociferous, garrulous, verbose, but never inarticulate, taciturn, or laconic. It's the quantity and continuity that are most conspicuous.

The adjective: *loquacious*

Can you match the words?

1. taciturn	a.	chattering meaninglessly
2. laconic	b.	wordy
3. inarticulate	c.	trite, hackneyed, unoriginal
4. garrulous	d.	fluent and rapid
5. banal	e.	noisy, loud
6. verbose	f.	spluttering unintelligibly
7. voluble	g.	talkative
8. cogent	h.	brilliantly compelling, persuasive
9. vociferous	i.	unwilling to engage in conversation
10. loquacious	j.	using few words packed with meaning

Key: 1-i, 2-j, 3-f, 4-a, 5-c, 6-b, 7-d, 8-h, 9-e, 10-g

Do you understand the words?

1. Do *taciturn* people usually make others
   feel comfortable and welcome?　　　　　　　　YES NO
2. Does a *laconic* speaker use more words than
   necessary?　　　　　　　　　　　　　　　　YES NO
3. Does rage make some people *inarticulate*?　　　YES NO
4. Is it interesting to listen to *garrulous* old men?　YES NO
5. Do *banal* speakers show a great deal of originality?　YES NO
6. Is *verbose* a complimentary term?　　　　　　　YES NO

7. Is it easy to be *voluble* when you don't know the
   subject you are talking about?   YES NO
8. Do unintelligent people usually make *cogent*
   statements?   YES NO
9. Is a *vociferous* demand ordinarily made by a shy,
   quiet person?   YES NO
10. Do *loquacious* people spend more
    time talking than listening?   YES NO

Key: 1-N, 2-N, 3-Y, 4-N, 5-N, 6-N, 7-N, 8-N, 9-N, 10-Y

SESSION 7 – MORE ABOUT HOLDING IT IN, LETTING IT OUT

1. About keeping one's mouth shut

If you let your mind play over some of the *taciturn* people you know,
you will realize that their abnormal disinclination to conversation
makes them seem morose, sullen, and unfriendly.

Taciturn (TAS'-i-tərn) is from a Latin verb *taceo*, to be silent, and is
one of those words whose full meaning cannot be expressed by any
other combination of syllables. It has many synonyms, among them
silent, uncommunicative, reticent, reserved, secretive, tight-lipped, and
close-mouthed; but no other word indicates the *permanent, habitual,*
and *temperamental* disinclination to talk implied by *taciturn*. The noun
is *taciturnity* (tas-i-TəRN'-i-ti).

2. Better left unsaid

Tacit (TAS'-it) derives also from *taceo*.

Here is a man dying of cancer. He suspects what his disease is, and
everyone else, of course, knows. Yet he never mentions the dread
word, and no one who visits him ever breathes a syllable of it in his
hearing. It is *tacitly* understood by all concerned that the word will
remain forever unspoken.

We speak of a *tacit* agreement, arrangement, acceptance, rejection,
assent, refusal, etc. A person is never called *tacit*.

The noun is *tacitness* (TAS'-it-nəs). (Bear in mind that you can
transform any adjective into a noun by adding *-ness*, though in many
cases there may be a more sophisticated, or more common, noun
form.)

Changing the *a* of the root *taceo* to *i*, and adding the prefix *re-*, again,
we can construct the English word *reticent* (RET'-i-sənt). Someone is

reticent who prefers to keep silent, whether out of shyness, embarrassment, or fear of revealing what should not be revealed. (The idea of 'againness' in the prefix has been lost in the current meaning of the word.) The noun form is *reticence* (RET'-i-səns).

3. Talk, talk, talk!

Loquacious (lə-KWAY'-shəs) people love to talk. This adjective is not necessarily a put-down, but the implication is that you wish such people would pause for breath once in a while so that *you* can have your turn. The noun is *loquacity* (lə-KWAS'-i-ti), or, of course, *loquaciousness*.

The word derives from Latin *loquor*, to speak, a root found also in:

1. *soliloquy* (sə-LIL'-ə-kwi) – a speech to oneself (*loquor* plus *solus*, alone), or, etymologically, a speech when alone. This word is applied to speeches made in a play by characters who are speaking their thoughts aloud to the audience. The *soliloquist* (sə-LIL'-ə-kwist) may be alone; or other members of the cast may be present on stage, but of course they don't hear what's being said, because they're not supposed to know. The verb is to *soliloquize* (sə-LIL'-ə-kwīz').

2. A *ventriloquist* (ven-TRIL'-ə-kwist) is one who can throw his voice. A listener thinks the sound is coming from some source other than the person speaking. The combining root is Latin *venter, ventris*, belly; etymologically, *ventriloquism* (ven-TRIL'-ə-kwiz-əm) is the art of 'speaking from the belly'. The adjective is *ventriloquistic* (ven-tril'-ə-KWIS'-tik) or *ventriloquial* (ven'-tri-LŌ'-kwi-əl).

3. *Colloquial* (kə-LŌ-kwi-əl) combines *loquor*, to speak, with the prefix *con*. When people speak together in conversation, their language is usually more informal and less rigidly grammatical than what you might expect in writing or in public addresses. *Colloquial* patterns are perfectly correct – they are simply informal, and suitable to everyday conversation.

A *colloquialism* (kə-LŌ'-kwi-ə-liz-əm), therefore, is a *conversational-style* expression, like 'He hasn't got any' or 'Who are you going with?' as contrasted to the formal or literary 'He has none' or 'With whom are you going?'.

4. A *circumlocution* (sər-kəm-lə-KYOO'-shən) is, etymologically, a 'talking around' (*circum-*, around). Any way of expressing an idea that is roundabout or indirect is *circumlocutory* (sər-kəm-LOK'-yə-tər'-i).

Review of etymology

Write in the space provided an English word that uses each prefix, root, or suffix.

1. *taceo*   to be silent   _____
2. *-ent*   adjective suffix   _____
3. *-ence, -ency*   noun suffix   _____
4. *loquor*   to speak   _____
5. *solus*   alone   _____
6. *-ist*   one who   _____
7. *venter, ventris*   belly   _____
8. *-ic*   adjective suffix   _____
9. *con-, col-,*
   com-, cor-*   with, together   _____
10. *-al*   adjective suffix   _____

Can you match the words?

1. taciturnity   a. fond of talking a lot
2. tacitness   b. talking, or a speech, 'to oneself'
3. circumlocution   c. art of throwing one's voice
4. loquacity   d. unwillingness to engage in conversation
5. soliloquy   e. informal expression used in everyday conversation
6. ventriloquism   f. state of being understood though not actually expressed
7. colloquialism   g. method of talking indirectly or in a roundabout way
8. loquacious   h. talkativeness
9. reticence   i. a person speaking to himself
10. soliloquist   j. unwillingness to talk

Key: 1-d, 2-f, 3-g, 4-h, 5-b, 6-c, 7-e, 8-a, 9-j, 10-i

Do you understand the words?

1. A *tacit* understanding is put into words   YES NO
2. Inhibited people are seldom *reticent* about expressing anger   YES NO
3. A *soliloquist* expresses his thoughts aloud   YES NO

* *Con-* is spelled *col-* before a root starting with *l*, *cor-* before *r*, and *com-* before *m*, *p* or *b*.

4. A *ventriloquial* performance on stage involves a
   dummy who appears to be talking   YES NO
5. A *colloquial* style of writing is ungrammatical   YES NO
6. *Circumlocutory* speech is direct and forthright   YES NO
7. *Inarticulate* people are generally given
   to *loquaciousness*   YES NO
8. A *soliloquy* is a dialogue   YES NO
9. *Taciturnity* makes a person seem friendly   YES NO
10. A *colloquialism* is inappropriate in a formal written
    context   YES NO

Key: 1-N, 2-N, 3-Y, 4-Y, 5-N, 6-N, 7-N, 8-N, 9-N, 10-Y

SESSION 8 – ROLLING ONWARD

1. A Spartan virtue

In ancient Sparta, originally known as *Laconia*, the citizens were hard-bitten, stoical, military-minded, and noted for their economy of speech. Legend has it that when Philip of Macedonia was storming the gates of Sparta (or Laconia), he sent a message to the besieged king saying. 'If we capture your city we will burn it to the ground.' A one-word answer came back: 'If.'

It is from the name *Laconia* that we derive our word *laconic* (lə-KON'-ik) – pithy, concise, economical in the use of words almost to the point of curtness; precisely the opposite of *verbose*.

We have learned that -*ness*, -*ity*, and -*ism* are suffixes that transform adjectives into nouns – and all three can be used with *laconic*:

. . . with characteristic *laconicness* (lə-KON'-ik-nəs)
. . . her usual *laconicity* (lak'-ə-NIS'-ə-ti)
. . . with, for him, unusual *laconicism*
       (lə-KON'-i-siz-əm)

2. Brilliant

Cogent (KŌ'-jənt) is a term of admiration. A *cogent* argument is well put, and above all convincing. *Cogency* (KŌ'-jən-si) shows a keen mind, an ability to think clearly and logically. The word derives from the Latin verb *cogo*, to drive together, compel, force. A *cogent* argument *compels* acceptance because of its logic, its appeal to one's reason.

3. Back to talk

Here are some more words based on *loquor*, to speak.

The *eloquent* (EL'-ə-kwənt) person speaks *out* (*e-*, from *ex-*, out), is expressive, fluent, or persuasive in language. The word is partially synonymous with *cogent*, but *cogent* implies irresistible logical reasoning while *eloquent* suggests the skilful use of language to move and arouse a listener.

Magniloquent (mag-NIL'-ə-kwənt) (*magnus*, large) and *grandiloquent* (gran-DIL'-ə-kwənt) (*grandis*, grand) are virtually identical in meaning. *Magniloquence* or *grandiloquence* is the use of high-flown, grandiose, even pompous language; home is *a place of residence*, for example, a doctor is a *member of the medical fraternity*, etc.

Loquacious, verbose, voluble, and *garrulous* people are all talkative; but each type, you will recall, has a special quality.

If you are *verbose*, you smother your ideas with excess words, especially pedantic ones. *Verbose* is from Latin *verbum*, word – the *verbose* person is wordy.

If you are *voluble*, you speak rapidly and fluently; you are vocal, verbal, and highly articulate. *Voluble* comes from Latin *volvo, volutus*, to roll – words effortlessly roll off the *voluble* speaker's tongue.

If you are *garrulous*, you talk constantly, and usually aimlessly and meaninglessly, about trifles. *Garrulous* derives from Latin *garrio*, to chatter – a *garrulous* talker chatters away like a monkey.

The suffix *-ness* can be added to all these adjectives to form nouns. Alternate noun forms end in *-ity*:

verbosity	(vər-BOS'-i-ti)
volubility	(vol'-yoo-BIL'-i-ti)
garrulity	(ga-ROO'-li-ti)

4. At large

Here are some more words based on *magnus*, large, big, great:

1. *Magnanimous* (mag-NAN'-i-məs) – big-hearted, generous, forgiving (etymologically, 'great-minded') (*magnus* plus *animus*, mind).

2. *Magnate* (MAG'-nayt) – a person of great power or influence.

3. *Magnify* – to make larger, or make seem larger (*magnus* plus *-fy* from *facio*, to make).

4. *Magnificent* – *magnus* plus *fic-*, from *facio*.

5. *Magnitude* – *magnus* plus the common noun suffix *-tude*, as in *fortitude, multitude, gratitude*, etc.

6. *Magnum* (as of champagne or wine) – a large bottle, generally twice the size of a standard bottle.

5.   Words, words, words!

Latin *verbum* is *word*. A *verb* is the important word in a sentence; *verbatim* (vər-BAY'-tim) is word-for-word (a *verbatim* report).

Verbal (vər-bəl), ending in the adjectival suffix -*al*, may refer either to a *verb*, or to words in general (a *verbal* fight); or it may mean, loosely, *oral* or *spoken*, rather than written (*verbal* agreement or contract); or, describing people ('she is quite *verbal*'), it may refer to a ready ability to put feelings or thoughts into words.

Verbiage (VəR'-bi-ij) has two meanings: an excess of words ('Such *verbiage*!'); or jargon (medical *verbiage*, military *verbiage*).

6.   Roll on, and on!

Volvo, volutus, to roll, the source of *voluble*, is the root on which many important English words are based.

   1. *Revolve* (ri-VOLV') – roll again (and again), or to keep turning round. (The prefix is *re*-, back or again.)

The noun is *revolution* (rev-ə-LOO'-shən), which can be one such complete rolling, or, by logical extension, a radical change of any sort, especially political. The adjective *revolutionary* (rev'-ə-LOO'-shən-ə-ri) introduces us to a new adjective suffix, -*ary*, as in *contrary, disciplinary, stationary, imaginary*, etc.

   2. *Involve* – etymologically, 'roll in' ('I didn't want to get *involved*!'). Noun: *involvement*.

   3. *Evolve* (i-VOLV') – etymologically, 'roll out' (*e*-, out); hence to unfold, or gradually develop ('The final plan *evolved* from some informal discussions'). Noun: *evolution*.

Review of etymology

Write in the space provided an English word that uses each prefix, root, or suffix.

1.	*Laconia*	Sparta	_____
2.	-*ism*	noun suffix	_____
3.	-*ence*	noun suffix	_____
4.	*magnus*	big	_____
5.	*volvo, volutus*	to roll	_____
6.	*garrio*	to chatter	_____
7.	-*fy*	to make	_____
8.	-*tude*	noun suffix	_____
9.	-*ary*	adjective suffix	_____
10.	*in*-	in	_____

Can you match the words?

1. laconicity		a.	floweriness, pompousness, or elegance in speech
2. eloquence		b.	incessant chatter with little meaning
3. magniloquence		c.	important or influential person
4. verbosity		d.	a gradual unfolding or development; a 'rolling out'
5. volubility		e.	'a rolling round'; radical change; political upheaval
6. garrulity		f.	great economy in speech
7. magnate		g.	fluency, ease, and/or rapidity of speech
8. revolution		h.	great, artistic, or emotional expressiveness
9. evolution		i.	wordiness
10. cogency		j.	persuasiveness through logic; keen-mindedness in reasoning

Key: 1-f, 2-h, 3-a, 4-i, 5-g, 6-b, 7-c, 8-e, 9-d, 10-j

Do you understand the words?

1. Is *laconicism* characteristic of a verbose speaker?	YES	NO
2. Does a *magniloquent* speaker use short, simple words?	YES	NO
3. Did humans *evolve* from ape-men?	YES	NO
4. Is an *eloquent* speaker interesting to listen to?	YES	NO
5. Do verbose people use a lot of *verbiage*?	YES	NO
6. Is *volubility* characteristic of an inarticulate person?	YES	NO
7. Does *verbosity* show a careful and economical use of words?	YES	NO
8. Is a *verbal* person usually inarticulate?	YES	NO
9. Is a *garrulous* person persuasive and logical?	YES	NO
10. Is a *magnanimous* person selfish and petty-minded?	YES	NO

Key: 1-N, 2-N, 3-Y, 4-Y, 5-Y, 6-N, 7-N, 8-N, 9-N, 10-N

SESSION 9 – RELATIVELY SPEAKING

1. Front and back – and uncles

As well as *ventriloquist,* etc., *venter, ventris,* belly, is also the root on which *ventral* (VEN'-trəl) and *ventricle* are built.

The *ventral* side of an animal, for example, is the front or belly side.

A *ventricle* (VEN'-tri-kəl) is a hollow organ or cavity, as one of the two chambers of the heart.

The adjective form of *ventricle* is *ventricular* (ven-TRIK'-yoo-lə), which may refer to a *ventricle,* or may mean *having a bellylike bulge.* Other adjectives are similarly formed: *vehicle – vehicular, circle – circular.*

The Latin word for *uncle* is *avunculus,* from which we get *avuncular* (ə-VUNG'-kyoo-lə), referring to an uncle. And because uncles are traditionally kindly, indulgent, and protective, anyone who behaves so towards another (usually younger) person is *avuncular* or acts in an *avuncular* capacity.

So we go back to *ventral.* If there's a front or belly side, anatomically, there must be a reverse – a back side. This is the *dorsal* (DAW'-səl) side, from Latin *dorsum,* the root on which the verb *endorse* (in-DAWS') is built. If you *endorse* a cheque, you sign it on the back side; if you *endorse* a plan, an idea, etc., you *back* it, you express your approval or support. The noun is *endorsement* (in-DAWS'-mənt).

2. The noise and the fury

We have already met *vociferous,* from Latin *vox, vocis,* voice, plus *fero,* to bear or carry. Its noun is *vociferousness* (vō-SIF'-ə-rəs-nəs); the verb is to *vociferate* (vō-SIF'-ə-rayt'). Can you form the noun derived from the verb?

3. To sleep or not to sleep – that is the question

The root *fero* is found also in *somniferous* (som-NIF'-ə-rəs), combined with *somnus,* sleep – it means bringing sleep. So a *somniferous* lecture is so dull and boring that it is sleep-inducing.

Tack on the negative prefix *in-* to *somnus* to construct *insomnia* (in-SOM'-ni-ə), the abnormal inability to fall asleep when sleep is required or desired. The unfortunate victim of this disability is an *insomniac* (in-SOM'-ni-ak), the adjective is *insomniac* or *insomnious* (in-SOM'-ni-əs). Add a different adjective suffix to *somnus* to derive *somnolent* (SOM'-nə-lənt), sleepy, drowsy. Can you construct the noun form of *somnolent*?

Combine *somnus* with *ambulo*, to walk, and you have *somnambulism* (som-NAM'-byoo-liz-əm), walking in one's sleep. A person who is a sleepwalker is a *somnambulist* (*-ist* is a common suffix for a person who does something).

4. A walkaway

An *ambulatory* (AM'-byoo-lət-ə-ri) patient is well enough to get out of bed and walk around. To *amble* (AM'-bəl) is to walk aimlessly; an *ambulance* is so called because originally it was composed of two stretcher-bearers who *walked* off the battlefield with a wounded soldier; and a *preamble* (PREE'-am-bəl) is, by etymology, something that 'walks before' (*pre-*, before, beforehand), hence an introduction or introductory statement, a *preamble* to the speech, etc.

Teaser questions for the amateur etymologist – 2

1. *Circum* is a prefix meaning *around*, as in *circumlocution*, *circumference*, *circumnavigation*, etc. Thinking of the root *scribo*, *scriptus*, to write, can you work out the word meaning *writing*, or *written material, around* (the edge of something)?

2. You know the roots *somnus* and *loquor*. Can you combine these two roots to form an adjective meaning *talking in one's sleep*? Can you write the noun form of this adjective?

3. A *somnambulist* walks in his sleep. What does a *noctambulist* do?

4. *Soporific*, combining *sopor*, sleep, with *fic-* (from *facio*), to make, means *inducing or causing sleep*. Use *somnus*, another root for sleep, to construct a word that has the same form and meaning as *soporific*.

5. *Perambulate* is *to walk through*. Use another Latin prefix to construct a verb meaning *to walk around*.

(*Answers in Chapter 11*)

---

5. Back to sleep

Somnus is one Latin word for sleep – *sopor* is another. A *soporific* (sop'-ə-RIF'-ik) lecture, speaker, style of delivery, etc. will put the audience to sleep (*fic-* from *facio*, to make), and a *soporific* is a sleeping pill.

6. Noun suffixes

You know that -ness can be added to any adjective to construct the noun form. Write the noun derived from *inarticulate*.

Another, and very common, noun suffix attached to adjectives is, as you have discovered, -*ity*. So the noun form of *banal* is either *banalness*, or, more commonly, *banality* (bə-NAL'-i-ti).

Bear in mind, then, that -*ness* and -*ity* are common noun suffixes attached to adjectives, and -*ion* (or -*ation*) is a noun suffix frequently affixed to verbs (to *articulate* – *articulation*; to *vocalize* – *vocalization*; to *perambulate* – *perambulation*.)

Review of etymology

Write in the space provided an English word that uses each prefix, root, or suffix.

1. *venter, ventris*	belly	_____
2. *avunculus*	uncle	_____
3. *dorsum*	back	_____
4. *somnus*	sleep	_____
5. -*ous*	adjective suffix	_____
6. *ambulo*	to walk	_____
7. -*ory*	adjective suffix	_____
8. *pre-*	before, beforehand	_____
9. -*ness*	noun suffix	_____
10. -*ity*	noun suffix	_____

Can you match the words?

1. ventral	a.	unable to fall asleep
2. dorsal	b.	pertaining to sleepwalking
3. somniferous	c.	drowsy
4. insomnious	d.	support; backing
5. somnolent	e.	walk aimlessly
6. somnambulistic	f.	like an uncle; kindly; protective
7. endorsement	g.	introduction
8. amble	h.	referring to the front or belly
9. preamble	i.	sleep-inducing
10. avuncular	j.	referring to the back side

Key: 1-h, 2-j, 3-i, 4-a, 5-c, 6-b, 7-d, 8-e, 9-g, 10-f

Do you understand the words?

1. Does an *insomniac* often need a *soporific*?   YES   NO
2. Does a *somnambulist* always stay in bed when
   asleep?   YES   NO
3. Are *ambulatory* patients bedridden?   YES   NO
4. Does a *preamble* come after another event?   YES   NO
5. Is the *dorsal* side of an animal at the front?   YES   NO
6. Is a *ventricle* a part of the heart?   YES   NO
7. Does an *avuncular* attitude indicate affection and
   protectiveness?   YES   NO
8. Is *vociferation* habitual with quiet, shy people?   YES   NO
9. Is a *somnolent* person wide awake?   YES   NO
10. Is a *somniferous* speaker stimulating and exciting?   YES   NO

Key: 1-Y, 2-N, 3-N, 4-N, 5-N, 6-Y, 7-Y, 8-N, 9-N, 10-N

CHAPTER 3
LIARS AND LYING

Why do people lie? To increase their sense of importance, to escape punishment, to gain an end that would otherwise be denied them, out of long-standing habit, or sometimes because they actually do not know the difference between fact and fancy. And, to come right down to it, can we always be certain what is true and what is false?

SESSION 10 – TEN SORTS OF LIARS

1. You don't fool even some of the people

Everybody knows your propensity for avoiding facts. You have built so unsavoury a reputation that only a stranger is likely to be misled – and then, not for long.

A *notorious* liar

2. To the highest summits of artistry

Rarely does anyone lie as convincingly or as artistically as you do. Indeed, your mastery of the art is so great that your lying is almost always crowned with success – and you have no trouble seducing an unwary listener into believing that you are telling gospel truth.

A *consummate* liar

3. Beyond redemption or salvation

You are impervious to correction. Often as you may be caught in your fabrications, there is no reforming you – you go right on lying despite the punishment, embarrassment, or unhappiness that your distortions of truth may bring upon you.

An *incorrigible* liar

4. Too old to learn new tricks

You are the victim of firmly fixed and deep-rooted habits. Telling untruths is as frequent and customary an activity as brushing your teeth in the morning, or having toast and coffee for breakfast, or lighting up a cigarette after dinner.

An *inveterate* liar

5. An early start

You have such a long history of persistent falsification that one can only suspect that your vice started when you were reposing in your mother's womb.

A *congenital* liar

6. No let-up

You never stop lying. While normal people lie on occasion, and often for special reasons, you lie continually – not occasionally or even frequently, but all the time.

A *chronic* liar

7. A strange disease

You are not concerned with the difference between truth and falsehood; you do not bother to distinguish fact from fantasy. Your lying is a disease that no antibiotic can cure.

A *pathological* liar

8. No regrets

You are completely without a conscience. No matter what misery your fabrications may cause your innocent victims, you never feel the slightest twinge of guilt.

An *unconscionable* liar

9. Smooth!

Possessed of a lively imagination and a ready tongue, you can distort facts as smoothly and as effortlessly as you can say your name. But you do not always get away with your lies. Ironically enough, it is your very smoothness that makes you suspect: your answers are too quick to be true.

A *glib* liar

10. Outstanding!

All your lies are vicious – calculatedly, predeterminedly, coldly, and advisedly vicious. In short, your lies are so outstandingly hurtful that people gasp in amazement and disgust at hearing them.

An *egregious* liar

Related meanings

These ten expressive adjectives are not restricted to lying or liars. Note their general meanings:.

1. *notorious*	well known for some bad quality – a *notorious* philanderer
2. *consummate*	perfect, highly skilled – *consummate* artistry at the keyboard
3. *incorrigible*	beyond reform – an *incorrigible* optimist
4. *inveterate* /ɪnˈvetrət/	long-accustomed, deeply habituated – an *inveterate* smoker
5. *congenital*	happening before or during birth – a *congenital* deformity
6. *chronic* /ˈkrɒnɪk/	going on for a long time, or occurring again and again – *chronic* appendicitis
7. *pathological*	diseased – a *pathological* condition
8. *unconscionable*	without pangs of conscience – *unconscionable* cruelty to children
9. *glib* /glɪb/	smooth, suspiciously fluent – a *glib* witness
10. *egregious* /ɪˈgriːdʒəs/	outstandingly bad or vicious – *egregious* error

appalling /əˈpɔːlɪŋ/

With the exception of *consummate* and *congenital*, all ten adjectives have strongly derogatory implications and are generally used to describe people, characteristics, or conditions we disapprove of.

abhorrent /əbˈhɒr(ə)nt/

Can you match the words?

1. notorious *h*	a. beyond reform
2. consummate *j*	b. continuing over a long period of time; recurring
3. incorrigible	c. diseased
4. inveterate	d. from long-standing habit
5. congenital *i*	e. suspiciously smooth
6. chronic	f. without conscience or scruples

7. pathological _c_   g. outstandingly bad or vicious
8. unconscionable _f_   h. unfavourably known
9. glib _e_   i. from birth
10. egregious _____   j. finished, perfect, artistic

Key: 1-h, 2-j, 3-a, 4-d, 5-i, 6-b, 7-c, 8-f, 9-e, 10-g

Do you understand the words?

1. Do people become _notorious_ for good acts?	YES	NO
2. Is Beethoven considered a _consummate_ musical genius?	YES	NO
3. If a criminal is truly _incorrigible_, is there any point in attempting rehabilitation?	YES	NO
4. Does an _inveterate_ smoker smoke only occasionally?	YES	NO
5. Is a _congenital_ deformity one that occurs late in life?	YES	NO
6. Is a _chronic_ invalid ill much of the time?	YES	NO
7. Is a _pathological_ condition normal and healthy?	YES	NO
8. If a person commits an _unconscionable_ act of cruelty, is there any regret, remorse or guilt?	YES	NO
9. Is a _glib_ talker awkward and hesitant in speech?	YES	NO
10. Is an _egregious_ error very bad?	YES	NO

Key: 1-N, 2-Y, 3-N, 4-N, 5-N, 6-Y, 7-N, 8-N, 9-N, 10-Y

SESSION 11 – NEW TRICKS FOR OLD DOGS

1. Well known

'Widely but unfavourably known' is the common definition for _notorious_ (nō-TAW'-ri-əs). So: _notorious_ liars, _notorious_ gamblers, _notorious_ thieves. The noun is _notoriety_ (nō-tə-Ī'-ə-ti). /nəvtə'rʌıti/

The derivation is from Latin _notus_, known, from which we also get _noted_. It is an interesting characteristic of some words that a change of syllables can alter the emotional impact. Thus, an admirer of certain business executives will speak of them as '_noted_ industrialists'; these same people's enemies will call them '_notorious_ exploiters'.

2. Plenty of room at the top

The top of a mountain is the _summit_, a word derived from Latin _summus_, highest, which also gives us the mathematical term _sum_, as in

/quintessential/

addition. A *consummate* artist has reached the very highest point of perfection; and to *consummate* (KON'-sə-mayt') a marriage or a business deal is, etymologically, to bring it to the highest point.

Note how differently *consummate* (kən-SUM'-ət *or* KON'-sə-mət), the adjective, can be pronounced, compared with the verb to *consummate* (KON'-sə-mayt').

To make a noun out of the adjective *consummate*, add either *-ness* or *-acy*; *consummateness* (kən-SUM'-ət-nəs) or *consummacy* (kən-SUM'-ə-si). The noun from the verb to *consummate* is *consummation* (kon'-sə-MAY'-shən).

3. No help

Call people *incorrigible* (in-KOR'-i-jə-bəl) if all efforts to correct or reform them are to no avail. Thus one can be an *incorrigible* criminal, an *incorrigible* optimist, or an *incorrigible* philanderer. The word derives from Latin *corrigo*, to correct or set straight, plus the negative prefix *in-*.

The noun is *incorrigibility* (in-kor'-i-jə-BIL'-ə-ti) or, alternatively, *incorrigibleness*.

4. Veterans

Inveterate (in-VET'-ə-rit) comes from Latin *vetus*, old, plus prefix *in-*, in (not *in* the negative prefix as in *incorrigible*). *Inveterate* liars have been lying for so long, and their habits are by now so deep-rooted, that one can scarcely remember when they ever told the truth.

The noun is *inveteracy* (in-VET'-ər-ə-si) or *inveterateness*.

A *veteran* is an old hand at the game, and therefore skilful. The word is both a noun and an adjective: a *veteran* at (or in) swimming or police work – or a *veteran* actor or diplomat.

5. Birth

Greek *genesis*, birth or origin, is the source of a great many English words.

Genetics (jə-NET'-iks) is the science that deals with the transmission of hereditary characteristics from parents to offspring. The scientist specializing in the field is a *geneticist* (jə-NET'-i-sist), the adjective is *genetic* (jə-NET'-ik). The particle containing a hereditary characteristic is a *gene* (JEEN).

Genealogy (jeen'-i-AL'-ə-ji) is the study of family trees or ancestral origins (*logos*, study). The practitioner is a *genealogist* (jeen'-i-AL'-ə-jist).

The *genital* (JEN'-i-təl), or sexual, organs are involved in the process of conception and birth. The *genesis* (JEN'-ə-sis) of anything is its beginning, and *Genesis*, the first book of the Old Testament, describes the creation, or birth, of the universe.

Congenital is constructed by combining the prefix *con-*, with or together, and the root *genesis*, birth. So a *congenital* defect, deformity, etc. occurs at some point during pregnancy or birth. *Hereditary* (he-RED'-i-tər'-i) characteristics, on the other hand, are acquired at the moment of conception.

Congenital is used both literally and figuratively. Literally, it means some medical abnormality occurring during gestation. Figuratively, it exaggerates, for effect, the early existence of some quality: *congenital* liar, *congenital* fear of the dark, etc.

Review of etymology

Write in the space provided an English word that uses each prefix, root, or suffix.

1.	*notus*	known	____
2.	*summus*	highest	____
3.	*corrigo*	to correct, set straight	____
4.	*vetus*	old	____
5.	*con-*	with, together	____
6.	*genesis*	birth, origin	____
7.	*logos*	science, study	____
8.	*in-*	negative prefix	____
9.	*in-*	in	____
10.	*-ary*	adjective suffix	____

Can you match the words?

1. notoriety	a. state of artistic height
2. to consummate (*v.*)	b. beginning, origin
3. consummacy	c. science of heredity
4. incorrigibility	d. bring to completion
5. genetics	e. study of ancestry
6. genealogy	f. referring to characteristics passed on to offspring by parents
7. genital	g. referring to the reproductive or sexual organs
8. genesis	h. ill fame

| 9. hereditary | i. particle that transmits hereditary characteristics |
| 10. gene | j. state of being beyond reform or correction |

Key: 1-h, 2-d, 3-a, 4-j, 5-c, 6-e, 7-g, 8-b, 9-f, 10-i

Do you understand the words?

1. Does *notoriety* usually come to perpetrators of mass murders? YES NO
2. Is *incorrigibility* in a criminal a sign that rehabilitation is possible? YES NO
3. Is a *geneticist* interested in your parents' characteristics? YES NO
4. Does *inveteracy* suggest that a habit is new? YES NO
5. When you *consummate* a deal, do you back out of it? YES NO
6. Is a *veteran* actress long experienced at her art? YES NO
7. Is a *genealogist* interested in your family origins? YES NO
8. Are the *genital* organs used in reproduction? YES NO
9. Is the *genesis* of something the final point? YES NO
10. Are *hereditary* characteristics derived from parents? YES NO

Key: 1-Y, 2-N, 3-Y, 4-N, 5-N, 6-Y, 7-Y, 8-Y, 9-N, 10-Y

SESSION 12 – OUT OF SIGHT, OUT OF TIME

1. Of time and place

A *chronic* liar lies constantly, again and again; a *chronic* invalid is ill time after time, repeatedly. The derivation of the word is Greek *chronos*, time. The noun form is *chronicity* (krə-NIS'-ə-ti).

An *anachronism* (ə-NAK'-rə-niz-əm) is someone or something out of time, belonging to a different era, either earlier or later. (The prefix *ana-*, like *a-*, is negative.) The adjective is *anachronous* (ə-NAK'-rə-nəs) or *anachronistic* (ə-nak'-rə-NIS'-tik). Read a novel in which a scene is supposedly taking place in the nineteenth century and imagine one of the characters turning on a TV set. An *anachronism*!

An *anachronism* is out of *time*; something out of *place* is *incongruous* (in-KONG'-groo-əs), a word combining the negative prefix *in-*, the prefix *con-*, with or together, and a Latin verb meaning to *agree* or *correspond*. For example, it would be *incongruous* to take a pet guinea-pig to church. The noun form of *incongruous* is *incongruity* (in-kəng-GRŌŌ'-ə-ti).

Chronological (kron-əl-LOJ'-i-kəl), in correct time order, comes from *chronos*. To tell a story *chronologically* is to relate the events in the time order of their occurrence. *Chronology* (krə-NOL'-ə-ji) is either a list of events in the time order in which they have occurred, or the science of the accurate dating of events (*logos*, science) – the expert in this field is a *chronologist* (krə-NOL'-ə-jist).

A *chronometer* (krə-NOM'-i-tə), combining *chronos* with *metron*, measurement, is a highly accurate timepiece, especially one used on ships. *Chronometry* (krə-NOM'-ə-tri) is the measurement of time – the adjective is *chronometric* (kron'-ə-MET'-rik).

Add the prefix *syn-*, together, plus the verb suffix *-ize*, to *chronos*, and you have constructed *synchronize* (SIN'-krə-nīz'), etymologically *to time together*, or to move or happen at the same time or rate, as for example in synchronized swimming. The adjective is *synchronous* (SIN'-krə-nəs); the noun form of the verb *synchronize* is *synchronization* (sin'-krə-nī-ZAY'-shən).

2. Disease, suffering, feeling

The Greek word *pathos*, suffering, gives us *pathology* (pə-THOL'-ə-ji), the science or study of disease. *Pathology* may also be any diseased or abnormal physical condition; in short, simply *disease*; hence *pathological*, meaning diseased. A *pathologist* (pə-THOL'-ə-jist) is an expert who examines tissue to diagnose disease.

Pathos occurs in some English words with the additional meaning of *feeling*. If you feel or suffer with someone, you are *sympathetic* (sim-pə-THET'-ik) – *sym-* is a respelling before the letter *p* of the Greek prefix *syn-*, with or together. The noun is *sympathy* (SIM'-pə-thi), the verb *sympathize* (SIM'-pə-thīz).

The prefix *anti-* means *against*. If you experience *antipathy* (an-TIP'-ə-thi) to people or things, you feel *against* them – you feel strong dislike or hostility. The adjective is *antipathetic* (an'-ti-pə-THET'-ik).

But you may have *no* feeling at all – you are *apathetic* (ap-ə-THET'-ik); *a-*, the negative prefix. The noun is *apathy* (AP'-ə-thi), as in moral *apathy*, etc.

On the other hand, you may be so sensitive or perceptive that you identify with another's feelings – you have *empathy* (EM'-pə-thi); you *empathize* (EM'-pə-thīz), you are *empathetic* (em-pə-THET'-ik), or, to use an alternative adjective, *empathic* (em-PATH'-ik). *Em-* is a respelling before the letter *p* of the Greek prefix *en-*, in.

Someone is *pathetic* (pə-THET'-ik) who is obviously suffering —
such a person may arouse sympathy or pity (or perhaps *antipathy?*) in
you. Things as well as people can be *pathetic*.

Telepathic (tel-ə-PATH'-ik) communication occurs when people
can feel each other's thoughts from a distance, when they have ESP.
The noun is *telepathy* (tə-LEP'-ə-thi), which is built by combining
pathos, feeling, with the prefix *tele-*, distance.

Review of etymology

Write in the space provided an English word that uses each prefix,
root, or suffix.

1.	*chronos*	time	_____
2.	*ana-, a-*	negative prefix	_____
3.	*con-*	with, together	_____
4.	*in-*	negative prefix	_____
5.	*logos*	science, study	_____
6.	*metron*	measurement	_____
7.	*syn-, sym-*	with, together	_____
8.	*pathos*	disease, suffering, feeling	_____
9.	*en-, em-*	in	_____
10.	*tele-*	distance	_____

Can you match the words?

1. chronicity	a. out of place
2. anachronism	b. timepiece; device that measures time very accurately
3. incongruous	c. condition of continual or repeated occurrence
4. chronology	d. act of occurring, or of causing to occur, at the same time
5. chronometer	e. calendar of events in order of occurrence
6. apathy	f. something, or someone, out of time
7. synchronization	g. lack of feeling
8. pathology	h. to share or understand another's feelings
9. sympathize	i. ESP; communication from a distance
10. telepathy	j. disease; study of disease

Key: 1-c, 2-f, 3-a, 4-e, 5-b, 6-g, 7-d, 8-j, 9-h, 10-i

Do you understand the words?

1. Are these dates in *chronological* order?
   1492, 1941, 1586?   YES   NO
2. Is *pathology* the study of healthy tissue?   YES   NO
3. Is *telepathic* communication carried on by
   telephone?   YES   NO
4. Does a *sympathetic* response show an understanding
   of another's feelings?   YES   NO
5. Is one *antipathetic* to things, ideas, or people one
   finds agreeable?   YES   NO
6. Do *apathetic* people react strongly?   YES   NO
7. Does an *empathic* response show identification with
   the feelings of another?   YES   NO
8. Is a swimsuit *incongruous* dress at a formal
   ceremony?   YES   NO
9. Is an *anachronistic* attitude up to date?   YES   NO
10. Are *synchronous* movements out of time with one
    another?   YES   NO

Key: 1-N, 2-N, 3-N, 4-Y, 5-N, 6-N, 7-Y, 8-Y 9-N, 10-N

SESSION 13 – PUTTING TWO AND TWO TOGETHER

1. Knowing

The Latin *scio*, to know, and *sciens*, knowing, are found in many
English words.

Unconscionable and *conscience* use these roots plus the prefix *con-*,
with, together.

Your *conscience* is your knowledge *with* a moral sense of right and
wrong; if you are *unconscionable*, your conscience is not (*un-*) working,
or you have no conscience. The noun form is *unconscionableness* or
unconscionabilty (un-kon'-shə-nə-BIL'-ə-ti).

Conscious, also from *con-* plus *scio*, is knowledge or awareness of
one's emotions or sensations, or of what is happening around one.

Science, from *sciens*, is systematized *knowledge* as opposed, for
example, to belief, faith, intuition, or guesswork.

Add Latin *omnis*, all, to *sciens*, to construct *omniscient* (om-NIS'-si-ənt),
all-knowing, possessed of infinite knowledge. The noun is *omniscience*
(om-NIS'-si-əns).

Add the prefix *pre-*, before, to *sciens*, to construct *prescient* (PRES'-si-ənt) – knowing about events *before* they occur, i.e., psychic, or possessed of unusual powers of prediction. The noun is *prescience* (PRES'-si-əns).

And, finally, add the negative prefix *ne-* to *sciens* to produce *nescient* (NES'-si-ənt), not knowing, or ignorant. Can you, by analogy with the previous two words, find the noun form of *nescient*?

Teaser questions for the amateur etymologist – 3

1. *Notify* and *notice* derive from the same root. Can you define these two words, again in the context of *known*? What do you suppose the verb suffix *-fy* of *notify* means? (Think also of *simplify*, *clarify*, *liquefy*, etc.)

2. You are familiar with the root *chronos*; the Greek word *graphein* means to *write*. Suppose you came across a device called a *chronograph* in your reading. Can you make an educated guess as to the meaning?

3. Recognizing the root *genesis* in the verb *generate*, how would you define the word?

How about *regenerate*? What does the prefix *re-* mean?

4. Recognizing the root *omnis* in *omnipotent* and *omnipresent*, can you define the words?

Recalling how we formed a noun from the adjective *omniscient*, write the noun forms of *omnipotent* and *omnipresent*.

5. Think of the negative prefix in *anachronism*; think next of the noun *aphrodisiac*. Can you construct a word for *that which reduces or eliminates sexual desire?* /æfrədizɪæk/

(*Answers in Chapter 11*)

---

2. Fool some of the people . . .

Glib is from an old English root that means *slippery*. *Glib* liars or *glib* talkers are smooth and slippery; they have ready answers and a persuasive air – but they fool only the most *nescient*, for their smoothness lacks sincerity and conviction.

The noun is *glibness* (GLIB'-nəs). (Gift of the gab) is different

3. Herds and flocks

Egregious (i-GREE'-jəs) is from Latin *grex, gregis*, herd or flock. An *egregious* lie, mistake, etc., is so exceptionally bad that it stands *out*

(*e-*, a shortened form of the prefix *ex-*, out) from the *herd* or *flock* of other bad things. The noun is *egregiousness* (i-GREE'-jəs-nəs).

A person who enjoys companionship, who likes to be with the herd, is *gregarious* (gri-GAIR'-i-əs). The noun is *gregariousness* (gri-GAIR'-i-əs-nəs).

Add the prefix *con-*, with, together, to *grex, gregis*, to get the verb *congregate* (KONG'-gri-gayt'); add the prefix *se-*, apart, to build the verb *segregate* (SEG'-ri-gayt'); add the prefix *ad-*, to, towards (*ad-* changes to *ag-* before a root starting with *g-*), to construct the verb *aggregate* (AG-ri-gayt').

When people gather *together* in a *herd* or *flock*, they *congregate*. The noun is *congregation* (con'-gri-GAY'-shən), one of the meanings of which is a religious 'flock'.

Put people or things apart from the *herd*, and you *segregate* them. Can you construct the noun by adding the suitable noun suffix?

Bring individual items to or towards the *herd* or *flock*, and you *aggregate* them. What is the noun form of this verb? The verb *aggregate* also means *to come together to* or *towards the herd*, that is, *to gather into a mass or whole*, or by extension, *to total or amount to*. So *aggregate*, another noun form, pronounced AG'-ri-gət, is a group of individuals considered as a whole, as in the phrase 'people in the *aggregate* . . .'

Review of etymology

Write in the space provided an English word that uses each prefix, root, or suffix.

1. *grex, gregis*	herd, flock	_____
2. *con-*	with, together	_____
3. *ad-, ag-*	to, towards	_____
4. *un-*	negative prefix	_____
5. *scio*	to know	_____
6. *sciens*	knowing	_____
7. *omnis*	all	_____
8. *pre-*	before	_____
9. *se-*	apart	_____
10. *-ion*	noun suffix added to verbs	_____

Can you match the words?

1.	unconscionability	a.	knowing nothing
2.	omniscience	b.	outstanding badness
3.	prescience	c.	religious group; a massing together
4.	nescient	d.	total; mass; whole
5.	glibness	e.	exclusion from the herd; a setting apart
6.	egregiousness	f.	infinite knowledge
7.	gregarious	g.	friendly; fond of mixing with people
8.	congregation	h.	lack of conscience
9.	segregation	i.	suspiciously smooth fluency
10.	aggregate (*n.*)	j.	foreknowledge

Key: 1-h, 2-f, 3-j, 4-a, 5-i, 6-b, 7-g, 8-c, 9-e, 10-d

Do you understand the words?

1. Is *unconscionability* one of the signs of the psychopath? YES NO
2. Can anyone be truly *omniscient*? YES NO
3. Does a *prescient* fear indicate some knowledge of the future? YES NO
4. Is *nescience* a result of learning? YES NO
5. Does *glibness* make someone sound sincere and trustworthy? YES NO
6. Is an *egregious* mistake a serious one? YES NO
7. Do *gregarious* people enjoy parties? YES NO
8. Do spectators *congregate* at sports events? YES NO
9. Do we *segregate* hardened criminals from the rest of society? YES NO
10. Is an *aggregation* of problems a whole mass of problems? YES NO

Key: 1-Y, 2-N, 3-Y, 4-N, 5-N, 6-Y, 7-Y, 8-Y, 9-Y, 10-Y

TEST I
HOW TO CHECK YOUR PROGRESS

I Etymology

Root	Meaning	Example
1. *via*	_____	obviate
2. *aequus (equ-)*	_____	equivocal
3. *malus*	_____	malign
4. *dico, dictus*	_____	malediction
5. *volo*	_____	malevolent
6. *militis*	_____	militant
7. *bonus, bene*	_____	benevolent
8. *fides*	_____	infidelity
9. *scribo, scriptus*	_____	subscribe
10. *nox, noctis*	_____	equinox
11. *dono*	_____	condone
12. *libra*	_____	equilibrium
13. *taceo*	_____	taciturn
14. *loquor*	_____	loquacious
15. *solus*	_____	soliloquy
16. *venter, ventris*	_____	ventral
17. *magnus*	_____	magniloquence
18. *verbum*	_____	verbatim
19. *volvo, volutus*	_____	voluble
20. *dorsum*	_____	endorse

II More etymology

Root	Meaning	Example
1. *vox, vocis*	_____	vocal
2. *fero*	_____	vociferous

3. *ambulo*	_____	somnambulist
4. *somnus*	_____	somnolent
5. *pre-*	_____	preamble
6. *notus*	_____	notorious
7. *summus*	_____	consummate
8. *vetus*	_____	inveterate
9. *genesis*	_____	congenital
10. *chronos*	_____	chronic
11. *pathos*	_____	empathy
12. *grex, gregis*	_____	egregious
13. *sciens*	_____	prescient
14. *omnis*	_____	omniscient
15. *ana-*	_____	anachronism
16. *tele-*	_____	telepathy
17. *se-*	_____	segregate
18. *metron*	_____	chronometry
19. *syn-*	_____	synchronize
20. *manus*	_____	manuscript

III Same or opposite?

1. disparage – praise	S	O
2. proscribe – prohibit	S	O
3. placate – irritate	S	O
4. taciturn – talkative	S	O
5. cogent – persuasive	S	O
6. equilibrium – balance	S	O
7. malign – slander	S	O
8. inarticulate – verbal	S	O
9. verbose – laconic	S	O
10. adulate – idolize	S	O
11. condone – approve	S	O
12. parity – equality	S	O
13. equanimity – excitability	S	O
14. iniquity – injustice	S	O
15. militant – passive	S	O
16. malefactor – wrongdoer	S	O
17. somnolent – wakeful	S	O
18. amble – wander	S	O
19. notorious – infamous	S	O
20. congenital – inborn	S	O

IV Matching

1. is a criminal
2. cannot sleep
3. talks to himself
4. scientist of inheritance
5. skilled old hand
6. studies family trees
7. studies the cause of diseases
8. rides a horse
9. sings a song
10. walks in his sleep

a. veteran
b. soliloquist
c. somnambulist
d. pathologist
e. insomniac
f. malefactor
g. genealogist
h. vocalist
i. equestrian
j. geneticist

V More matching

1. horse-like
2. listless, feeling nothing
3. incapable of reform
4. saying two things at once
5. mindlessly talkative
6. noisy, clamorous
7. generous, forgiving
8. economical of speech
9. having the highest skill
10. doing good

a. equivocal
b. garrulous
c. consummate
d. beneficent
e. apathetic
f. equine
g. vociferous
h. magnanimous
i. incorrigible
j. laconic

VI Recall a word

1. ruthless; without conscience   U _____
2. suspiciously smooth-talking   G _____
3. outstandingly bad; vicious   E _____
4. out of place   I _____
5. study of the family tree   G _____
6. science of heredity   G _____
7. in correct order of time   C _____
8. diseased; pertaining to the study
   of disease (*adj.*)   P _____
9. measurement of time   C _____
10. to cause to occur at the same time   S _____
11. ignorant   N _____
12. knowledge of an occurrence beforehand P _____
13. enjoying companionship   G _____

14. to identify strongly with the feelings of another E _____
15. to speak to oneself, as in a play S _____
16. unselfish; not revengeful M_____
17. able to walk after being bedridden A _____
18. inability to fall asleep I _____
19. to make unnecessary O _____
20. not fond of chatter T _____

ANSWERS

Score 1 point for each correct answer.

I Etymology

1-road, 2-equal, 3-bad, evil, 4-to say, tell, 5-to wish, 6-soldier, 7-good, well, 8-faith, 9-to write, 10-night, 11-to give, 12-balance, pound, 13-to be silent, 14-to speak, 15-alone, 16-stomach, 17-big, great, 18-word, 19-to turn, 20-back
Your score?

II More etymology

1-voice, 2-to carry, 3-to walk, 4-sleep, 5-before, 6-known, 7-highest, 8-old, 9-birth, beginning, origin, 10-time, 11-feeling, 12-herd, 13-knowing, 14-all, 15-against, 16-far, at a distance, 17-apart, 18-measurement, 19-together, 20-hand
Your score?

III Same or opposite?

1-O, 2-S, 3-O, 4-O, 5-S, 6-S, 7-S, 8-O, 9-O, 10-S, 11-S, 12-S, 13-O, 14-S, 15-O, 16-S, 17-O, 18-S, 19-S, 20-S
Your score?

IV Matching

1-f, 2-e, 3-b, 4-j, 5-a, 6-g, 7-d, 8-i, 9-h, 10-c
Your score?

V More matching

1-f, 2-e, 3-i, 4-a, 5-b, 6-g, 7-h, 8-j, 9-c, 10-d
Your score?

VI   Recall a word

1-unconscionable, 2-glib, 3-egregious, 4-incongruous, 5-genealogy, 6-genetics, 7-chronological, 8-pathological, 9-chronometry, 10-synchronize, 11-nescient, 12-prescience, 13-gregarious, 14-empathize, 15-soliloquize, 16-magnanimous, 17-ambulant, 18-insomnia, 19-obviate, 20-taciturn
Your score?

Now add up your score over the whole test. The maximum possible score is 100 points.

90–100	Masterly work; you have a talent for words
80–89	Good work; you are making very satisfactory progress
60–79	Average work; could you improve your study technique?
40–59	Not up to standard; work harder
20–39	Poor; you need to revise before going on
0–19	Why are you doing so badly?

CHAPTER 4
HOW TO INSULT YOUR ENEMIES

Psychology makes clear that loving and being loved are important elements in emotional health, but also points out the necessity for expressing, rather than repressing, our hostilities. It is a mark of your emotional maturity if you can find the most accurate words to describe the faults that you find in other people.

SESSION 14 – TEN WAYS OF BEING BAD

1. Slave driver

She makes everyone toe the line. She exacts blind, unquestioning obedience and demands the strictest conformity to rules, however arbitrary or tyrannical. She is the very epitome of the army drill sergeant.

She is a *martinet*.

2. Toady

You pander to rich or influential people. All your servile attention and unceasing adulation spring from your own selfish desires to get ahead, not out of any sincere admiration.

You are a *sycophant*.

3. Dabbler

Often a person of independent income, he engages superficially in the pursuit of one of the fine arts – painting, composing, etc. He does this largely for his own amusement and not to achieve any professional competence. His artistic efforts are simply a means of passing time pleasantly.

He is a *dilettante*.

4. Bogus

He tries to gain advantage or position by pretending to have qualifications that he has not got, or to know people he does not really know.

He is an *impostor*.

5. Superpatriot

Anything you belong to is better – your religion is far superior, your political party is the only honest one, your neighbourhood puts all others in the city in the shade. Above all, your country is the finest in the world.

You are a *chauvinist*.

6. Fanatic

He has a one-track mind – he has such an excessive zeal for one thing (children, food, money, or whatever) that his obsession is almost absurd.

He is a *monomaniac*.

7. Attacker

She is violently against established beliefs, revered traditions, cherished customs – such, she says, stands in the way of reform and progress and are always based on superstition and irrationality.

She is an *iconoclast*.

8. Sceptic

There is no God – that is their position and they will not budge from it.

They are *atheists*.

9. Sexual pest

He is lascivious, libidinous, lustful, lewd, wanton, immoral – he promiscuously attempts to satisfy (and is often successful in so doing) his sexual desires with any woman within arm's reach.

He is a *lecher*.

10. Worrier

You are always ill, though no doctor can find a cause for your ailments. As you travel from doctor to doctor, futilely seeking confirmation of your fatal disease, you become convinced that you're too weak to go on much longer. Organically, of course, there's nothing the matter with you.

You are a *hypochondriac*.

Can you match the person with the characteristic?

1. martinet	a. superficiality
2. sycophant	b. patriotism
3. dilettante	c. godlessness
4. impostor	d. single-mindedness
5. chauvinist	e. anti-tradition
6. monomaniac	f. sex
7. iconoclast	g. illness
8. atheist	h. discipline
9. lecher	i. bogus credentials
10. hypochondriac	j. flattery

Key: 1-h, 2-j, 3-a, 4-i, 5-b, 6-d, 7-e, 8-c, 9-f, 10-g

Do you understand the words?

1. Does a *martinet* condone carelessness?	YES	NO
2. Is a *sycophant* a sincere person?	YES	NO
3. Is a *dilettante* a hard worker?	YES	NO
4. Is an *impostor* genuine and trustworthy?	YES	NO
5. Is a *chauvinist* modest and self-effacing?	YES	NO
6. Does a *monomaniac* have a one-track mind?	YES	NO
7. Does an *iconoclast* scoff at tradition?	YES	NO
8. Does an *atheist* believe in God?	YES	NO
9. Is a *lecher* virtuous?	YES	NO
10. Does a *hypochondriac* have a lively imagination?	YES	NO

Key: 1-N, 2-N, 3-N, 4-N, 5-N, 6-Y, 7-Y, 8-N, 9-N, 10-Y

SESSION 15 – A FIG FOR THE GREEKS

1. The French drillmaster

Jean Martinet was the Inspector-General of Infantry during the reign of Louis XIV – and a stricter, more fanatic drillmaster France had never seen. It is from his name that we derive our English word *martinet* (mah-ti-NET'). It is always used in a derogatory sense and generally shows resentment and anger on the part of the user.

2. A Greek 'fig-shower'

Sycophant comes from two Greek words, *sykon*, fig, and *phanein*, to show. Originally it meant the person who informed the officers in charge when (1) the figs in the sacred groves at Smyrna were being taken, or (2) when the fig-dealers were dodging the tariff. Thus, a *sycophant* (SIK'-ə-fant) is a sort of 'grass'. By extension, sycophants use flattery or servile attentions to insinuate themselves into someone's good graces. A *sycophant* practices *sycophancy* (SIK'-ə-fan-si), and has a *sycophantic* (sik-ə-FAN'-tik) attitude. All three forms of the word are highly uncomplimentary.

Material may be so delicate or fine in texture that anything behind it will show through. The Greek prefix *dia-* means *through*; and *phanein*, as you now know, means *to show* – hence such material is called *diaphanous* (dī-AF'-ə-nəs).

3. Just for one's own amusement

Dilettante is from the Italian verb *dilettare*, to delight. The *dilettante* (dil'-ə-TAN'-ti) paints, composes, or engages in scientific experiments purely for amusement – not to make money, become famous, or satisfy a deep creative urge. A *dilettantish* (dil-i-TAN'-tish) attitude is superficial, unprofessional; *dilettantism* (dil-i-TAN'-tiz-əm) is the related noun.

Do not confuse the *dilettante* with the *tyro* (TĪ'-rō), who is the inexperienced beginner in some art, but who may be full of ambition, drive, and energy. On the other hand, anyone who has developed consummate skill in an artistic field, generally allied to music, is called a *virtuoso* (vər'-tyōō-Ō'-zō) – like Evelyn Glennie on percussion. Pluralize *virtuoso* in the normal way – *virtuosos*; or if you wish to sound more sophisticated, give it the continental form – *virtuosi* (vər'-tyōō-Ō'-si). Similarly, the plural of *dilettante* is either *dilettantes* or *dilettanti* (dil-ə-TAN'-ti).

4. False pretences

Impostor is from the Latin *in-*, in, and *pono*, to place. An *impostor* (im-POS'-tə) is someone who positions himself – but falsely. A similar word is *charlatan* (SHAH'-lə-tən), which can also denote someone pretending to have medical qualifications; it comes from the Italian *ciarlare*, to chatter.

5. The old man

Nicolas Chauvin, soldier of the French Empire, so vociferously aired his veneration of Napoleon Bonaparte that he became the laughing-stock of all Europe. Thereafter, a fanatical patriot was known as a *chauvinist* (SHŌ'-vi-nist). *Chauvinism* (SHŌ'-və-niz-əm) also applies to blatant veneration of, or boastfulness about, any other affiliation besides one's country.

To be *patriotic* (pat-ri-O'-tik) is to be normally proud of one's country – to be *chauvinistic* (shō-və-NIS'-tik) is to exaggerate such pride to an obnoxious degree. *Patriotic* is built on the Latin word *pater, patris,* father – one's country is, in a sense, one's fatherland.

Other interesting words are built on this same root:

1. *patrimony* (PAT'-ri-mō-ni) – an inheritance from one's father. The *-mony* comes from the same root that gives us *money,* namely *Juno Moneta,* the Roman goddess who guarded the temples of finance. The adjective is *patrimonial* (pat'ri-MŌ'-ni-əl).

2. *patronymic* (pat'-rə-NIM'-ik) – a name formed on the father's name, like *Johnson* (son of John). The word combines *pater, patris* with Greek *onyma,* name. *Onyma* plus the Greek prefix *syn-,* with or together, forms *synonym* (SIN'-ə-nim), a word of the same meaning, for example *hate/detest. Onyma* plus the prefix *anti-,* against, forms *antonym* (AN'-tə-nim), a word of opposite meaning. *Onyma* plus Greek *homos,* the same, forms *homonym* (HOM'-ə-nim), where the words are spelt the same but have different meanings, such as *bear/ bear.* Distinguish this from a *homophone* (HOM'-ə-fōn), a combination of *homos,* the same, and *phone,* sound, when two words sound the same but have different meanings and spellings, like *way/weigh.* The adjective form of *synonym* is *synonymous* (si-NON'-i-məs). Can you write the adjectives derived from *antonym, homonym,* and *homophone.*

3. *paternity* (pə-TəR'-ni-ti) – fatherhood; the adjective is *paternal* (pə-TəR'-nəl), fatherly. *Paternalism* (pə-TəR'-nə-liz-əm) is the philosophy of governing a country, or of managing a business, so that the citizens or employees are treated in a manner suggesting a father–children relationship. It is now used as a term of disapproval. The adjective is *paternalistic* (pə-tər'-nə-LIS'-tik).

4. *patriarch* (PAY'-tri-ahk') – an old man in a ruling, fatherlike position. Here *pater, patris* is combined with the Greek root *archein,* to rule. The adjective is *patriarchal* (pay'-tri-AHR'-kəl), the system is a *patriarchy* (PAY'-tri-ah'-ki).

5. *patricide* (PAT'-ri-sīd') – the killing of one's father. *Pater, patris* combines with *-cide,* a suffix derived from the Latin verb *caedo,* to kill. The adjective is *patricidal* (pat-ri-SĪ'-dəl).

6. The old lady

Mater, matris is Latin for *mother,* and it too has many derivatives:

1. *matriarch* (MAY'-tri-ahk') – the mother-ruler; the 'mother person' that controls a large household, tribe, or country. Again the root is *archein,* to rule. During the reign of Queen Victoria, England was a *matriarchy* (MAY'-tri-ah'-ki). Can you work out the adjective form?

2. *maternity* (mə-TəR'-ni-ti) – motherhood.

3. *maternal* (mə-TəR'-nəl) – motherly.

4. *matron* (MAY'-trən) – an older married woman, one sufficiently mature to be a mother. The adjective is *matronly* (MAY'-trən-li), and it has slightly uncomplimentary overtones.

5. *alma mater* (AL'-mə-MAH'-tə *or* AL'-mə-MAY'-tə) – 'cherishing mother'; actually, the school or college which one attended, and which in a sense is one's intellectual mother.

6. *matrimony* (MAT'-ri-mə-ni) – marriage. Though this word is similar to *patrimony* in spelling, it does not refer to *money* – the noun suffix *-mony* indicates state or result, as in *sanctimony, parsimony*, etc. The adjective is *matrimonial* (mat'-ri-MŌ'-ni-əl).

7. *matricide* (MAT'-ri-sīd') *or* (MAY'-tri-sīd') – the killing of one's own mother. The adjective?

7. Murder most foul . . .

There is a word for almost every kind of killing you can think of:

1. *suicide* (SOO'-i-sīd') – killing oneself (intentionally); Latin *sui*, of oneself, plus *-cide*.

2. *fratricide* (FRAT'-ri-sīd') – the killing of one's brother; Latin *frater, fratris*, brother, plus *-cide*.

3. *sororicide* (sə-ROR'-i-sīd') – the killing of one's sister; Latin *soror*, sister, plus *-cide*.

4. *homicide* (HOM'-i-sīd') – the killing of a human being; Latin *homo*, person, plus *-cide*. In law, *homicide* is the general term for any slaying. If intent and premeditation can be proved, the act is *murder* and punishable as such. If no such intent is present, the act is called *manslaughter* and receives a lighter punishment.

5. *genocide* (JEN'-ō-sīd') – the killing of a whole race or nation. This is a comparatively new word, coined in 1944 to refer to the mass murder of the Jews, Poles, etc. ordered by Hitler. Derivation: Greek *genos*, race, kind, plus *-cide*.

In all these cases, the noun refers both to the crime itself and to the person who perpetrates it. The adjective always ends *-cidal*, e.g. *suicidal*.

Review of etymology

Write in the space provided an English word that uses each prefix, root, or suffix.

1. *phanein*	to show	_____
2. *pater, patris*	father	_____
3. *syn–*	with, together	_____
4. *onyma*	name	_____
5. *homos*	the same	_____
6. *archein*	to rule	_____
7. *mater, matris*	mother	_____
8. *-mony*	noun suffix	_____
9. *sui*	oneself	_____
10. *genos*	race, kind	_____

Can you match the words?

1. sycophancy	a.	fervent patriot
2. patricide	b.	one's school or college
3. matriarch	c.	the same in sound but not in spelling or meaning
4. chauvinist	d.	similar in meaning
5. alma mater	e.	toadying
6. diaphanous	f.	killing of one's father
7. synonyms	g.	murder
8. antonyms	h.	filmy, gauzy
9. homicide	i.	mother–ruler
10. homophones	j.	opposite in meaning

Key: 1-e, 2-f, 3-i, 4-a, 5-b, 6-h, 7-d, 8-j, 9-g, 10-c

Do you understand the words?

1. Is a *paternalistic* manager kind to his staff? YES NO
2. Does *dilettantism* show firmness and tenacity? YES NO
3. Is a *tyro* particularly skilful? YES NO
4. Is a violin *virtuoso* an accomplished musician? YES NO
5. Is a *synonym* a form of flattery? YES NO
6. Does a substantial *patrimony* obviate financial insecurity? YES NO
7. If you know a person's *patronymic* can you deduce his father's name? YES NO
8. Do *homonyms* sound the same? YES NO
9. Does a *matriarch* have a good deal of power? YES NO
10. Does *fratricide* mean murder of one's sister? YES NO

Key: 1-Y, 2-N, 3-N, 4-Y, 5-N, 6-Y, 7-Y, 8-Y, 9-Y, 10-N

SESSION 16 – MONARCHY AND MADNESS

1. All in the family

Frater, brother; *soror*, sister; *uxor*, wife; and *maritus*, husband – these roots are the source of a number of additional English words:

1. to *fraternize* (FRAT'-ə-nīz') – to have a brotherly relationship (with). It denotes having a social relationship with one's subordinates (of either sex) in an organization, as in, 'The head of the college was reluctant to *fraternize* with faculty members.' The verb gained a new meaning during and after World War II, when soldiers of occupying armies had sexual relations with the women of conquered countries, as in, 'Military personnel were strictly forbidden to *fraternize* with the enemy.'

Can you write the noun form of *fraternize*?

2. *fraternal* (frə-TəR'-nəl) – brotherly. The word also designates *non-identical* twins.

3. *fraternity* (frə-TəR'-ni-ti) – a brotherhood or guild, or any group of people of similar interests or profession (the medical *fraternity*).

4. *sorority* (sə-ROR'-i-ti) – a women's organization, especially one in an American school or college.

5. *uxorious* (uk-SAW'-ri-əs) – an adjective describing a man who excessively, even absurdly, dotes on his wife. This word is *not* synonymous with *henpecked*, as the henpecked husband fears and is dominated by his wife.

6. *uxorial* – pertaining to, characteristic of, or befitting, a wife, as *uxorial* duties, privileges, attitudes, etc.

7. *marital* (MAR'-i-təl) – pertaining or referring to, or characteristic of, a husband; but the meaning has changed to include the marriage relationship of both husband *and* wife, as *marital* duties obligations, privileges, arguments, etc. Hence *extra-marital* is literally *outside the marriage*, as in *extramarital* affairs (sex with someone other than one's spouse). And *premarital* (Latin prefix *pre-*, before) describes events that occur before a planned marriage, as a *premarital* agreement as to the division of property, etc.

2. Of cabbages and kings (without the cabbage)

Rex, regis is Latin for *king*. *Tyrannosaurus rex* was the king (i.e. the largest) of the dinosaurs (etymologically, 'king of the tyrant lizards'). And *regal* (REE'-gəl) is royal, or fit for a king, hence magnificent, stately, imperious, splendid, etc., as in *regal* bearing or manner, a *regal* mansion, etc. The noun is *regality* (ree-GAL'-i-ti). *Regalia* (ri-GAYL'-iə), a plural noun, originally designated the emblems of a king, and now refers to any impressively formal clothes or to the decorations, insignia, or uniform of a rank or office.

3. 'Madness' of all sorts

The *monomaniac* develops an abnormal obsession in respect to *one* particular thing (Greek *monos*, one), but is otherwise normal. The obsession itself, or the obsessiveness, is *monomania* (mon'-ō-MAY'-ni-ə), the adjective is *monomaniacal* (mon'-ō-mə-NĪ'-ə-kəl).

Psychology recognizes many other abnormal states with names built on Greek *mania*, madness:

1. *dipsomania* (dip'-sō-MAY'-ni-ə) – a morbid compulsion to keep on absorbing alcoholic beverages; alcoholism (Greek *dipsa*, thirst. Adjective: *dipsomaniacal* (dip'-sō-mə-NĪ'-ə-kəl).

2. *kleptomania* (klep'tō-MAY'-niə) – a morbid compulsion to steal, not from any economic motive, but simply because the urge to take another's possessions is irresistible. The *kleptomaniac* (Greek *klepte*, thief) may be wealthy, and yet be an obsessive shoplifter. Adjective: *kleptomaniacal* (klep'-tō-mə-NĪ'-ə-kəl).

3. *pyromania* (pī'-rō-MAY'-ni-ə) – morbid compulsion to start fires. *Pyromania* should not be confused with *incendiarism* (in-SEN'-di-ə-riz-əm), which is the malicious burning of another's property. Some *pyromaniacs* heroically put out the very blaze they themselves have started, whereas an *incendiary* (in-SEN'-di-ə-ri) is antisocial and usually starts fires for revenge. In law, setting fire to property for an improper purpose, such as collecting on an insurance policy, is called *arson* (AH'-sən) and is a criminal act. The *pyromaniac* sets fire to property for the thrill; the *incendiary* for revenge; the *arsonist* (AH'-sə-nist) for money.

Pyromania is built on Greek *pyros*, fire; *incendiarism* on Latin *incendo, incensus*, to set fire; *arson* on Latin *ardo, arsus*, to burn.

4. *megalomania* (meg'-ə-lō-MAY'-ni-ə) – morbid delusions of grandeur, power, importance, godliness, etc. (Greek *megas*, great, large).

Can you think of the word for an instrument that someone speaks through to make the *sound* (*phone*) of his voice *greater*?

4. And now phobias

There are people who have irrational and deep-seated dread of cats, dogs, fire, snakes, thunder or lightning, various colours, and so on almost without end.* Such morbid dread or fear is called a *phobia*, from the Greek *phobos*, fear.

---

* For some of these esoteric phobias, see Appendix.

1. *claustrophobia* (klaw'-strə-FŌ'-bi-ə *or* klo'-strə-FŌ'bi-ə) – morbid dread of being physically hemmed in, of enclosed spaces, of crowds, etc. (Latin *claustra*, enclosed place). The person: *claustrophobe* (KLAW'-strə-fōb' *or* KLO'-strə-fōb'). Adjective: *claustrophobic* (klaw-strə-FŌ'-bik *or* klo'-strə-FŌ'-bik).

2. *agoraphobia* (ag'-ə–rə-FŌ'-bi-ə) – morbid dread of open space, the reverse of *claustrophobia* (Greek *agora*, market place). People suffering from *agoraphobia* prefer to stay shut up in their homes as much as possible, and may become panic-stricken in public places. The person? The adjective?

3. *acrophobia* (ak'-rə-FO'-biə) – morbid dread of high places (Greek *akros*, highest). The victims of this fear will not climb ladders, and they refuse to go on to the roof of a building or look out the window of one of the higher floors. The person? The adjective?

Review of etymology

Write in the space provided an English word that uses each prefix, root, or suffix.

1. *frater, fratris*	brother	_____
2. *uxor*	wife	_____
3. *maritus*	husband	_____
4. *monos*	one	_____
5. *-ac*	noun suffix 'one who'	_____
6. *klepte*	thief	_____
7. *pyros*	fire	_____
8. *ardo, arsus*	to burn	_____
9. *mega*	great, large, big	_____
10. *akros*	highest	_____

Can you match the words?

1. dipsomania	a. women's society
2. acrophobia	b. excessively fond of one's wife
3. uxorial	c. delusions of grandeur
4. kleptomania	d. insignia of rank or office
5. incendiarism	e. characteristic of a wife
6. megalomania	f. compulsive stealing
7. uxorious	g. fear of enclosed spaces
8. regalia	h. alcoholism

| 9. claustrophobia | i. fear of heights |
| 10. sorority | j. maliciously starting fires |

Key: 1-h, 2-i, 3-e, 4-f, 5-j, 6-c, 7-b, 8-d, 9-g, 10-a

Do you understand the words?

1. Is an *uxorious* husband psychologically dependent on his wife? YES NO
2. Are *extramarital* affairs adulterous? YES NO
3. Do VIPs often receive *regal* treatment? YES NO
4. Do *monomaniacal* people have varied interests? YES NO
5. Do people of *pyromaniacal* tendencies fear fire? YES NO
6. Is *incendiarism* an uncontrollable impulse? YES NO
7. Would an *agoraphobe* be comfortable in a small cell-like room? YES NO
8. Does an *acrophobe* enjoy mountain-climbing? YES NO
9. Do members of a *fraternity* have interests in common? YES NO
10. Is an *arsonist* a criminal? YES NO

Key: 1-Y, 2-Y, 3-Y, 4-N, 5-N, 6-N, 7-Y, 8-N, 9-Y, 10-Y

SESSION 17 – GOD AND KNOWLEDGE

1. No reverence

The *iconoclast* sneers at convention and tradition, and attempts to expose as shams our cherished beliefs. Adolescence is that rebellious time of life for *iconoclasm* (ī-KON'-ə-klaz'-əm) – indeed the adolescent who is not *iconoclastic* (ī-kon'-ə-KLAST'-ik) to some degree is unusual. The words are from the Greek *eikon*, a religious image, plus *klaein*, to break.

2. Is there a God?

Atheist combines the Greek negative prefix *a-* with *theos*, God. Do not confuse *atheism* (AY'-thi-iz-əm) with *agnosticism* (ag-NOS'-ti-siz-əm), the philosophy that claims that God is unknowable. The *atheist* denies the existence of God, the *agnostic* (as-NOS'-tik) holds that no proof can be adduced one way or the other. *Agnostic* (which is also an adjective) is built on the Greek root *gnostos*, known, and the negative prefix *a-*.

3. How to know

A *diagnosis* (dī-əg-NŌ'-sis), constructed on the allied Greek root *gnosis*, knowledge, plus *dia-*, through, is a knowing through examination or testing. A *prognosis* (prog-NŌ'-sis) is, etymologically, a knowing beforehand, hence a prediction, generally as to the course of a disease (Greek prefix *pro-*, before, plus *gnosis*).

The verb form of *diagnosis* is *diagnose* (DĪ'-əg-nōz' *or* dī'-əg-NŌZ'); the verb form of *prognosis* is *prognosticate* (prog-NOS'-ti-kayt').

The medical specialist in *diagnosis* is a *diagnostician* (dī'-əg-nos-TISH'-ən).

The noun form of the verb *prognosticate* is *prognostication* (prog-nos'-ti-KAY'-shən).

4. Getting back to God

The Greek word *theos*, God, is also found in:

1. *Monotheism* (MON'-ō-thee'-iz-əm) – belief in *one* God (Greek *monos*, one). Using *atheism, atheist*, and *atheistic* as a model, find the word for the person who believes in one God; and the adjective.

2. *Polytheism* (POL'-i-thee-iz-əm) – belief in *many* gods, as in ancient Greece or Rome (Greek *poly*, many).

Teaser questions for the amateur etymologist – 4

1. If a *patronymic* is a name derived from the name of one's father, can you work out the word for a name derived from one's *mother*'s name?

2. *Incendo, incensus*, to set on fire, is the origin of the adjective *incendiary*, the noun *incense*, and the verb *to incense*. (a) What is an *incendiary* statement or speech? (b) Why do people use *incense*, and why is it called *incense*? (c) If somebody *incenses* you, or if you feel *incensed*, how does the meaning of the verb derive from the root?

3. *Ardo, arsus*, to burn, is the source of *ardent* and *ardour*. Explain these two words in terms of the root.

4. What is used to make sound greater (use of the roots for *great* and *sound*)?

5. A *metropolis*, by etymology, is the mother city (Greek *méter*, mother, plus *polis*, city, state). Construct a word for a *great city* (think of *megalomania*, delusions of greatness).

(Answers in Chapter 11) •

3. *Pantheism* (PAN'-thi-iz-əm) – belief that God is not in man's image, but is a combination of all forces of the universe (Greek *pan*, all).

4. *Theology* (thee-OL'-ə-ji) – the study of God and religion (Greek *logos*, science or study). The student is a *theologian* (thee'-ə-LŌ-jən), the adjective is *theological* (thee'-ə-LOJ'-i-kəl).

5.   Under and over

Hypochondria (hī-pə-KON'-dri-ə) is built on two Greek roots: *hypo*, under, below, and *chondros*, the cartilage of the breastbone. The ancient Greeks believed that morbid anxiety about one's health arose in the abdomen, which is below the breastbone.

Hypochondriac is both a noun and an adjective, with an alternative adjectival form, *hypochondriacal* (hī-pə-kon-DRĪ'-ə-kəl).

Hypo, under, is a useful root to know. The *hypodermic* needle penetrates *under* the skin (Greek *derma*, skin); a *hypothyroid* person has an *underworking* thyroid gland; *hypotension* is abnormally low blood pressure.

On the other hand, *hyper* is the Greek root meaning *over*. The *hypercritical* person is excessively fault-finding; *hyperthyroidism* is an overworking of the thyroid gland; *hypertension* is high blood pressure; and you can easily work out the meanings of *hyperactive*, *hypersensitive*, etc.

Be careful with words beginning *hypo-* or *hyper-* – one may be the antonym of the other.

Review of etymology

Write in the space provided an English word that uses each prefix, root, or suffix.

1. *eikon*	religious image	_____
2. *a–*	negative prefix	_____
3. *theos*	God	_____
4. *-ic*	adjective suffix	_____
5. *gnosis*	knowledge	_____
6. *poly*	many	_____
7. *logos*	science, study	_____
8. *-al*	adjective suffix	_____
9. *hypo*	under	_____
10. *hyper*	over	_____

Can you match the words?

1.	hypotension	a.	excessive fault-finding
2.	iconoclasm	b.	view that God is unknowable
3.	pantheism	c.	study of religion
4.	hypochondria	d.	belief that God is in nature
5.	agnosticism	e.	ascertainment by examination or testing
6.	hypercritical	f.	morbid anxiety about health
7.	diagnosis	g.	denial of existence of God
8.	theology	h.	a foretelling of future developments
9.	prognosis	i.	abnormally low blood pressure
10.	atheism	j.	contempt for tradition

Key: 1-i, 2-j, 3-d, 4-f, 5-b, 6-a, 7-e, 8-c, 9-h, 10-g

Do you understand the words?

1.	An *atheist* studies the origins of religion	YES NO
2.	Young people are usually *iconoclasts*	YES NO
3.	A *diagnostician* is a kind of priest	YES NO
4.	My *hypercritical* boss is easily pleased	YES NO
5.	The ancient Greeks were *polytheists*	YES NO
6.	*Agnostics* do not believe in God	YES NO
7.	Nowadays breast cancer has a good *prognosis*	YES NO
8.	*Hypochondria* is a serious condition	YES NO
9.	*Hypertension* is a serious condition	YES NO
10.	Is a *theologian* necessarily a Christian?	YES NO

Key: 1-N, 2-Y, 3-N, 4-N, 5-Y, 6-N, 7-Y, 8-N, 9-Y, 10-N

Baffled?

You are learning to work out the meaning of a word from its
origins. But do not be surprised if sometimes you cannot do it:
English contains many, many words whose origins are unknown
(and *baffled* is one of them!).

mahogany – the reddish-brown wood from a rainforest tree
nifty – neat and smart
bamboozle – to undertake a fancy sort of swindle
dapple – the colour of many rocking-horses
oodles – plenty of what?
theodolite – nothing to do with God, it is a surveyor's instrument
oche – the line you throw from in darts
clobber – the clothes you wear, or hitting someone over the head
boffin – the backroom genius
boost – a helpful push; what your vocabulary is getting right now

CHAPTER 5
HOW TO FLATTER YOUR FRIENDS

Words are the symbols of emotions, as well as ideas. You can show your feeling by the tone you use ('You're silly' can be an insult, an accusation, or an endearment, depending on how you say it) or by the words you choose. Consider the interesting types of people described in the following paragraphs, then note how accurately the adjective applies to each type.

SESSION 18 – TEN WAYS OF BEING GOOD

1. Put the kettle on, Polly

They are friendly, happy, extroverted, and gregarious – the sort of people who will invite you out for a drink, who like to transact business around the lunch table, who offer coffee as soon as company drops in.
    The adjective is: *convivial*

2. You can't tire them

We all have the same amount of time – twenty-four hours a day. It's not time that counts but energy. Some people apparently have boundless, illimitable energy – they're on the go from morning to night, and often far into the night, working hard, playing hard, never tiring – and getting twice as much done as any three other human beings.
    The adjective is: *indefatigable*

3. No tricks, no secrets

They are pleasingly frank, utterly lacking in pretence or artificiality, in fact quite unable to hide their feelings or thoughts. They have something of the simple naturalness and unsophistication of a child.
    The adjective is: *ingenuous*

4. The eagle's eye

They have minds as sharp as razors; their insight into problems that would mystify people of less keenness or discernment is just short of amazing.

The adjective is: *perspicacious*

5. No placating necessary

They are most generous about forgiving a slight or an injury. Never do they harbour resentment, store up petty grudges, or waste energy on thoughts of revenge or retaliation.

The adjective is: *magnanimous*

6. One-person orchestras

The range of their aptitudes is formidable. If they are artists, they use oils, water colours, gouache, charcoal, pen and ink – anything! If they are musicians, they can play strings, wind, keyboards – everything! Such people can turn their hands to whatever is needed.

The adjective is: *versatile*

7. No grumbling

They bear their troubles bravely, never ask for sympathy, never yield to sorrow, never wince at pain.

The adjective is: *stoical*

8. No fear

There is not a cowardly bone in their bodies. They are strangers to fear, they're audacious, dauntless, contemptuous of danger and hardship.

The adjective is: *intrepid*

9. No dullness

They are witty, clever, amusing; and they excel as conversationalists.

The adjective is: *scintillating*

10. City slickers

They are cultivated, poised, tactful, sophisticated, and courteous, at ease under all social circumstances. You cannot help admiring their self-assurance.

The adjective is: *urbane*

Can you match the words?

1. convivial	a. frank
2. indefatigable	b. unflinching
3. ingenuous	c. noble
4. perspicacious	d. capable in many directions
5. magnanimous	e. tireless
6. versatile	f. fearless
7. stoical	g. keen-minded
8. intrepid	h. witty
9. scintillating	i. friendly
10. urbane	j. polished, sophisticated

Key: 1-i, 2-e, 3-a, 4-g, 5-c, 6-d, 7-b, 8-f, 9-h, 10-j

Do you understand the words?

1. convivial – hostile	S	O
2. indefatigable – tireless	S	O
3. ingenuous – worldly	S	O
4. perspicacious – obtuse	S	O
5. magnanimous – petty	S	O
6. versatile – all-rounder	S	O
7. stoical – unemotional	S	O
8. intrepid – timid	S	O
9. scintillating – banal	S	O
10. urbane – rude	S	O

Key: 1-O, 2-S, 3-O, 4-O, 5-O, 6-S, 7-S, 8-O, 9-O, 10-O

SESSION 19 – THE HIGH LIFE

1.   Eat, drink and be merry

The Latin verb *vivo*, to live, and the noun *vita*, life, are the source of a number of important English words.

Convivo is the Latin verb *to live together*; from this we get our English word *convivial* (kon-VIV'-i-əl), an adjective that describes the kind of person who likes to go out and enjoy himself with good company.

Using the suffix *-ity* can you write the noun form of the adjective *convivial*?

2. Living it up

Among many others, the following English words derive from Latin *vivo*, to live:

1. *vivid* (VIV'-id) – possessing the freshness of life; strong; sharp – a *vivid* colour. Add *-ness* to form the noun.

2. *revive* (ri-VĪV') – bring back to life. Noun: *revival* (ri-VĪ'-vəl).

3. *vivacious* (vī-VAY'-shəs) – lively, high-spirited. Nouns: *vivacity* (vī-VAS'-i-ti) or *vivaciousness*.

4. *viva* (VĪ'-və) – an examination in the form of an interview. It is short for *viva voce*, with a live voice (Latin *vox, vocis*, voice).

3. Which came first?

Latin *ovum*, egg, is the source of *oval* and *ovoid*, egg-shaped; *ovulate* (O'-vyoo-layt'), to release an egg from the *ovary*; and *ovum* (Ō'-vəm), the female germ cell which, when fertilized by a sperm, develops into an embryo, then into a *foetus* (FEE'-təs), and finally, in about 280 days in the case of humans, is born as an infant.

The adjectival form of *ovary* is *ovarian* (ō-VAIR'-i-ən); of *foetus*, *foetal* (FEE'-təl). Can you write the noun form of the verb *ovulate*?

Love also comes from *ovum*. No, not the kind of love you're thinking of. *Ovum* became *oeuf* in French, or with 'the' preceding the noun (*the egg*), *l'oeuf*, pronounced something like LəRF. *Zero* is shaped rather like an egg (0), so if your score in tennis is *fifteen* and your opponent's is *zero*, you shout triumphantly, 'fifteen love!'.

4. More about life

Latin *vita*, life, is the origin of:

1. *vitamin* – one of the nutritional elements essential for the body's metabolism. For example, good eyesight requires vitamin A (found in vegetables, especially carrots).

2. *vital* (VĪ'-təl) – essential to life; of crucial importance, full of life and vigour. Add the suffix *-ity* to form the noun.

3. *Revitalize* (ree-VĪ'-tə-līz') is constructed from the prefix *re-*, again, back, the root *vita*, and the verb suffix. It means to restore vitality, to rejuvenate.

4. The prefix *de-* has a number of meanings, one of which is essentially negative, as in *defrost, decompose, declassify*, etc. Using this prefix, can you find the verb meaning *to rob of life, to take life from*?

Vitalize, revitalize, and *devitalize* are used figuratively – for example, a programme or plan is *vitalized, revitalized*, or *devitalized*, according to how it's handled.

5. French life

Sometimes, instead of getting our English words directly from Latin, they come to us via a European language, usually French. Here are two French phrases based on the Latin root *vivo*, to live.

1. *joie de vivre* (zhwah'-də-VEEV'). Literally *joy of living*, this phrase describes an immense delight in being alive, an effervescent keenness for all the daily activities that human beings can indulge in. The opposite is *ennui* (on-WEE'), a feeling of boredom, discontent with life.

2. *bon vivant* (BON'-vee-VONH' – the -NH a muted nasal sound. A *bon vivant* is a person who lives luxuriously, especially in respect to rich food, good drink, opera-going, etc. It means, literally, a *good living*. The *bon vivant* is, of course, a *convivial* person.

6. More good things

French *bon*, good, is from Latin *bonus* (see Session 5). Here are some other words based on it:

1. *bonhomie* (BON'-ə-mī), good-natured friendliness. From French *homme*, man, so literally good-man-ness.

2. *bon voyage* (bonh vwah-YAHZH'). Have a good journey!

Review of etymology

Write in the space provided an English word that uses each prefix, root, or suffix.

1. *vivo*	to live	_____
2. *-ous*	adjective suffix	_____
3. *re-*	again, back	_____
4. *ovum*	egg	_____
5. *vita*	life	_____
6. *-ize*	verb suffix	_____
7. *de-*	negative prefix	_____
8. *bon*	good	_____
9. *-ate*	verb suffix	_____
10. *-oid*	adjective suffix	_____

Can you match the words?

1. conviviality	a. release of the egg
2. vivacious	b. one who lives lavishly

3. devitalize	c. strong; sharp
4. ovulation	d. egg-shaped
5. vitality	e. effervescence; joy of living
6. *joie de vivre*	f. take life from
7. ennui	g. high-spirited
8. bon vivant	h. boredom
9. vivid	i. love of good company
10. ovoid	j. strength, vigour

Key: 1-i, 2-g, 3-f, 4-a, 5-j, 6-e, 7-h, 8-b, 9-c, 10-d

Do you understand the words?

1. conviviality – bonhomie	S	O
2. vivacious – apathetic	S	O
3. vivid – dull	S	O
4. oval – square	S	O
5. revitalize – rejuvenate	S	O
6. ennui – boredom	S	O
7. *bon vivant* – 'man about town'	S	O
8. vitality – liveliness	S	O
9. *bon voyage* – hello	S	O
10. *joie de vivre* – boredom	S	O

Key: 1-S, 2-O, 3-O, 4-O, 5-S, 6-S, 7-S, 8-S, 9-O, 10-O

SESSION 20 – SIMPLICITY AND BELIEVING

1. No fatigue

Indefatigable is a derived form of *fatigue* – *in-* is a negative prefix, the suffix *-able* means *able to be*; hence, literally, *indefatigable* means *unable to be fatigued*. The noun is *indefatigability* (in'-di-fat'-i-gə-BIL'-i-ti).

2. How simple can one be?

Ingenuous is a complimentary term, though its synonyms *naive*, *gullible*, and *credulous* are faintly derogatory.

To call people *ingenuous* (in-JEN'-yoo-əs) implies that they are frank, open, and not likely to try to put anything over on you.

Ingenuous should not be confused with *ingenious* (in-JEEN'-i-əs) – note the difference in spelling – which on the contrary means *shrewd*, *clever, inventive.* The noun form of *ingenuous* is *ingenuousness*; of *ingenious, ingenuity* (in'-ji-NYOO'-i-ti) or ingeniousness.

To call people *naive* (nī-EEV') is to imply that they have not learned the ways of the world, and are therefore trusting beyond the point of safety. The noun is *naivety* (nī-EEV'-ə-ti).

Credulous (KRED'-yoo-ləs) implies a willingness to believe almost anything, no matter how fantastic. *Credulity* (kri-DYOO'-li-ti), like *naivety*, usually results from ignorance or inexperience.

Gullible (GUL'-ə-bəl) means *easily fooled* or *easily imposed on*. It is a stronger word than *credulous* and is more derogatory. *Gullibility* (gul'-ə-BIL'-i-ti) results more from stupidity than from ignorance or inexperience.

3. Belief and disbelief

Credulous comes from Latin *credo*, to believe, the same root found in *credit* (if people *believe* in your honesty, they will extend *credit* to you; they will *credit* what you say). *-ous* is an adjective suffix that usually signifies *full of*. So, strictly, *credulous* means *full of believingness*.

Do not confuse *credulous* with *credible* (KRED'-i-bəl). In the latter word we see combined the root *credo*, believe, with *-ible*, a suffix meaning *can be*. Something *credible* can be believed.

Let's note some differences:

Credulous listeners – those who fully believe what they hear.

A *credible* story – one that can be believed.

An *incredulous* (in-KRED'-yoo-ləs) attitude – an attitude of scepticism, of non-belief.

An *incredible* (in-KRED'-i-bəl) story – one that cannot be believed.

Nouns are formed as follows:

credulous – *credulity* (kri-DYOO-li-ti)
incredulous – *incredulity* (in-kri-DYOO-li-ti)
credible – *credibility* (kred'-i-BIL'-i-ti)
incredible – *incredibility* (in-kred'-i-BIL'-i-ti)

4. What people believe in

Credo, to believe, is the origin of four other useful English words.

1. *Credo* (KREE'-dō *or* KRAY'-dō) – personal belief, code of ethics.

2. *Creed* – a religious belief, such as Catholicism, Judaism, Protestantism, Hinduism, etc.

3. *Credence* (KREE'-dəns) – belief, as in, 'I place no *credence* in his stories'.

4. *Credentials* (kri-DEN'-shəls) – a document or documents giving evidence of a person's standing.

5. Heads and tails

If *ingenuous* means *frank, open*, then *disingenuous* (dis-in-JEN'-yoo-əs) should mean *not frank or open*. But *disingenuous* people are far more than simply *not ingenuous*. They are crafty, dishonest, insincere – and they are all of these while making a pretence of being frank and above-board. Like a wolf in sheep's clothing. Similarly, a remark may be *disingenuous*, as may also a statement, an attitude, a confession, etc. The noun is *disingenuousness*.

Review of etymology

Write in the space provided an English word that uses each prefix, root, or suffix.

1. *in-*	negative prefix	_____
2. *-ness*	noun suffix	_____
3. *credo*	to believe	_____
4. *-ous*	adjective suffix	_____
5. *-ible*	can be; able to be	_____
6. *-ity*	noun suffix	_____
7. *-ence*	noun suffix	_____
8. *dis-*	negative prefix	_____
9. *-ulous*	adjective suffix	_____
10. *-ibility*	noun suffix	_____

Can you match the words?

1. ingenious   a. easily tricked
2. credulous   b. religious belief
3. gullible   c. inexperienced; unworldly
4. incredible   d. document proving identity
5. creed   e. unbelievable
6. credentials   f. shrewdness; cleverness
7. ingenuity   g. clever; inventive; shrewd
8. naive   h. willing to believe

Key: 1-g, 2-h, 3-a, 4-e, 5-b, 6-d, 7-f, 8-c

Can you use the words correctly?

Use *credulous, credible,* or corresponding negative or noun forms in the following sentences:

1. She listened _____ly to her husband's confession of his frequent infidelity, for she had always considered him a paragon of moral uprightness.
2. He told his audience an _____ and fantastic story of his narrow escapes.
3. He'll believe you – he's very _____.
4. Make your characters more _____ if you want your readers to believe in them.
5. We listened dumb-struck, full of _____, to the shocking details of corruption and vice.
6. He has the most _____ good luck.
7. The _____ of it! How can such things happen?
8. Naive people accept with complete _____ whatever anyone tells them.
9. 'Do you believe me?' 'Sure – your story is _____ enough.'
10. I'm not objecting to the total _____ of your story, but only to your thinking that I'm _____ enough to believe it!

Key: 1-incredulously,   2-incredible,   3-credulous,   4-credible, 5-incredulity,   6-incredible,   7-incredibility,   8-credulity,   9-credible, 10-incredibility, credulous

---

SESSION 21 – A PIERCING GLANCE

1. How to look

The Latin root *specto,* to look, is the source of many common English words: *spectacle, spectator, inspect, retrospect* (a looking back), *prospect* (a looking ahead), etc. In a variant spelling, *spic-,* the root is found in *conspicuous* (easily seen or looked at), *perspicacious,* and *perspicuous.*

A *perspicacious* (pər'-spi-KAY'-shəs) person is keen-minded and astute. *Per-* is a prefix meaning *through*; so the word means *looking through* (matters, etc.) keenly. The noun is *perspicacity* (pər'-spi-KAS'-i-ti) or *perspicaciousness.*

Perspicacity has a synonym *acumen* (AK'-yoo-mən), mental keenness, keen insight. The root is Latin *acuo,* to sharpen.

2. Sharpness

From *acuo*, to sharpen, come such words as *acute*, sharp, sudden, as *acute* pain, *acute* reasoning, etc; and *acupuncture* (AK'-yoo-pungk'-chə), the insertion of a (sharp) needle into the body for medical purposes. The noun form of *acute*, referring to the mind or vision, is *acuteness* or *acuity* (ə-KYOO'-i-ti); in other contexts, *acuteness* only.

Acupuncture combines *acuo*, to sharpen, with *punctus*, point. When you *punctuate* a sentence, you put various *points* (full stops, commas, etc.) where needed. If you are *punctual*, you're right on the point of time (noun: *punctuality*); if you're *punctilious* (pungk-TIL'-i-əs), you are very careful to observe the proper *points* of behaviour, procedure, etc. (noun: *punctiliousness*). And to *puncture* something, of course, is to make a hole in it with a sharp *point*. *Pungent* (PUN'-jənt) comes from another form of the root *punctus* (*pungo*, to pierce sharply), so a *pungent* smell is sharp or spicy, pricking the nose; and a *pungent* wit sharply pierces one's sense of humour. The noun is *pungency* (PUN'-jən-si), *not* pungentness.

3. Some more looking

Perspicacious should not be confused with *perspicuous* (pə-SPIK'-yoo-əs). Here is the important distinction:

Perspicacious means *able to look through and understand quickly*. This adjective applies to persons, their reasoning, minds, etc.

Perspicuous is the other side of the coin – it means *easily understood from one look*, and applies to writing, style, books, and like things that have to be understood. Hence it is a synonym of *clear, simple, lucid*.

The noun form of *perspicuous* is *perspicuity* (pər'-spi-KYOO'-i-ti), or *perspicuousness*.

A *spectacle* is something to *look at*; *spectacles* (glasses) are the means by which you get a comfortable and accurate *look* at the world. Anything *spectacular* is, etymologically, worth *looking* at.

A *spectator* is one who *looks* at what's happening.

To *inspect* is to *look into* something.

Retrospect (RET'-rō-spekt') is a backward *look* (*retro*, backward) – generally the word is preceded by the preposition *in*, for instance, 'Most experiences seem more enjoyable *in retrospect* than in actuality'.

Prospect (PROS'-pekt) is a forward *look*; *prospective* (prə-SPEK'-tiv) is the adjective. What's the *prospect* for world peace? Similarly, your *prospective* job or holiday is the activity in the future that you look forward to. (The prefix is *pro-*, forward, ahead, before.)

If you *introspect* (in'-trə-SPEKT'), you look inwards and examine your inner reactions (the prefix is *intro-*, inwards). Too much *introspection* (in'-trə-SPEK'-shən) or *introspectiveness* may lead to feelings of anxiety.

There are times when you have to look *around* most carefully; you must then be *circumspect* (SəR'-kəm-spekt') – watchful, cautious, alert (*circum-*, around). The noun is *circumspection* (sər'-kəm-SPEK'-shən) or *circumspectness*.

If something looks good or sensible, but actually is not, we call it *specious* (SPEE'-shəs). A *specious* argument sounds plausible, but in reality is based on an error, a fallacy, or an untruth. The noun is *speciousness*.

Review of etymology

Write in the space provided an English word that uses each prefix, root, or suffix.

1.	*specto*	to look	_____
2.	*per-*	through	_____
3.	*acuo*	to sharpen	_____
4.	*punctus*	point	_____
5.	*pungo*	to pierce sharply	_____
6.	*-ence, -ency*	noun suffixes	_____
7.	*retro-*	backward	_____
8.	*pro-*	forward, ahead, before	_____
9.	*intro-*	inside, within	_____
10.	*circum-*	around	_____

Can you match the words?

1.	perspicacious	a.	extremely careful, exact, or proper in procedure
2.	acumen	b.	clear; easy to understand
3.	specious	c.	a forward look
4.	punctilious	d.	looking inside
5.	pungent	e.	keen-minded
6.	perspicuous	f.	sharp; spicy; piercing
7.	retrospect	g.	wary, cautious, 'looking around'
8.	prospect	h.	sharpness of mind or thinking
9.	introspective	i.	a backward look
10.	circumspect	j.	plausible but actually false

Key: 1-e, 2-h, 3-j, 4-a, 5-f, 6-b, 7-i, 8-c, 9-d, 10-g

Do you understand the words?

1. perspicacious – dull witted		S	O
2. acumen – stupidity		S	O
3. acute – sharp		S	O
4. acuity – perspicacity		S	O
5. punctilious – casual		S	O
6. pungent – bland		S	O
7. perspicuous – clear		S	O
8. retrospect – backward look		S	O
9. circumspect – careless		S	O
10. specious – true		S	O

Key: 1-O, 2-O, 3-S, 4-S, 5-O, 6-O, 7-S, 8-S, 9-O, 10-O

SESSION 22 – CITY SLICKERS, COUNTRY CLOWNS

1. The great and the small

You are familiar with Latin *animus*, mind. *Animus* and a related root, *anima*, life principle, soul, spirit, are the source of such words as *animal, animate* and *inanimate, animated,* and *animation.*

Magnanimous (meaning generous-minded) contains, in addition to *animus*, mind, the root *magnus*, large, great; the noun is *magnanimity* (mag'-nə-NIM'-i-ti).

On the other hand, people who have tiny minds or souls are *pusillanimous* (pyōo'-si-LAN'-i-məs) – Latin *pusillus*, tiny. Hence they are contemptibly petty and mean. The noun is *pusillanimity* (pyōo'-si-lə-NIM'-i-ti).

Other words built on *animus*, mind, include:

1. *unanimous* (yōo-NAN'-i-məs) – of one *mind*. If the judges of a competition are *unanimous*, they are all of *one* mind. (Latin *unus*, one.) The noun is *unanimity* (yōo-nə-NIM'-i-ti).

2. *equanimity* (ee'-kwə-NIM'-i-ti *or* ek'-wə-NIM'-i-ti) – equal (or balanced) mind. Hence, evenness or calmness of mind; composure. If you preserve your *equanimity* under trying circumstances, you do not get confused, you remain calm. (Latin *aequus*, equal.)

3. *animus* (AN'-i-məs) – hostility, ill will. Etymologically, *animus* is simply *mind*, but has degenerated to mean *unfriendly mind*: 'I bear you no *animus*, even though you have tried to destroy me'.

4. *animosity* (an'-i-MOS'-ə-ti) – ill will, hostility. An exact synonym of *animus*, and a more common word. 'There is real *animosity* between Bill and Ernie'.

Teaser questions for the amateur etymologist – 5

1. Recalling the root *vivo*, to live, how would you explain a *vivarium*?

2. *Unus* is Latin for *one*. Can you use this root to construct words meaning:

(a)   animal with *one* horn: _____
(b)   of *one* form: _____
(c)   to make *one*:   _____
(d)   *one*ness: _____
(e)   *one*-wheeled vehicle: _____

3. *Annus* is Latin for *year*; *verto*, *versus*, as you know, means *to turn*. Can you explain the word *anniversary* in terms of its roots?

4. Use *inter-*, between, to form words of the following meanings:

(a)   *between* states (*adj*.):   _____
(b)   *between* nations (*adj*.):   _____
(c)   *between* persons (*adj*.):   _____

5. Use *intra-*, within, to form words with the following meaning (all *adjectives*):

(a)   *within* one state: _____
(b)   *within* one nation: _____
(c)   *within* the muscles: _____

(*Answers in Chapter 11*)

---

2. Turning

Versatile comes from *verto*, *versus*, to turn – *versatile* people can turn their hand to many things successfully. The noun is *versatility* (vər'-sə-TIL'-i-ti).

3. Zeno and the front porch

In ancient Greece, the philosopher Zeno used to lecture on 'How to Live a Happy Life'. Zeno would stand on a porch (the Greek word for which is *stoa*) and expound his credo as follows: people should free themselves from intense emotion, be unmoved by both joy and sorrow, and submit without complaint to unavoidable necessity. His followers were called *Stoics*, after the *stoa*, or porch, from which the master lectured.

If we call people *stoical* (STŌ'-ik-əl), we mean that they meet adversity with unflinching fortitude. *Stoicism* (STŌ'-i-siz-əm) may be an admirable virtue (mainly because we do not then have to listen to the *stoic*'s troubles), but it can be overdone.

4. Fear and trembling

Intrepid is from Latin *trepido*, to tremble. (You recognize the negative prefix *in-*.) *Intrepid* people exhibit fearlessness (and not a single tremble!) when confronted by dangers. The noun: *intrepidity* (in'-trə-PID'-i-ti), or, of course, *intrepidness*.

Trepido is also the source of *trepidation* (trep'-i-DAY'-shən) – great fear, trembling, or alarm.

5. Quick flash

Scintilla, in Latin, is a spark from a fire; in English the word *scintilla* (sin-TIL'-ə) may also mean a *spark*, but more commonly refers to a very small particle (which, in a sense, a spark is), as in, 'There was not a *scintilla* of evidence against him'.

In the verb *scintillate* (SIN'-ti-layt'), the idea of the spark remains; someone who *scintillates* sparkles with charm and wit. The noun is *scintillation* (sin'-ti-LAY'-shən).

6. City and country

People who live in the big city go to theatres, attend the opera, visit museums and art galleries, browse in book shops, and shop at designer boutiques. These activities fill them with culture and sophistication. (Also they have the privilege of spending two hours a day going to and coming from work.) As a result, city-dwellers are refined, polished, courteous – or so the etymology of *urbane* (from Latin *urbs*, city) tells us. The noun is *urbanity* (ər-BAN'-i-ti).

Urban (əR'-bən) as an adjective simply refers to cities – *urban* populations, *urban* life, *urban* development, etc.

The *suburbs* are residential sections, or small communities, close to a large city. (*Sub-* has a number of meanings: *under, near, close to*, etc.) *Suburbia* (sə-BəR'-bi-ə) may designate *suburbs* as a group; *suburban* residents, or *suburbanites* (sə-BəR'-bə-nīts'), as a group.

Latin *rus, ruris* is the country, i.e. farmland, fields, etc. So *rural* (ROOəR'-əl) refers to country or farm regions, agriculture, etc.

Rustic (RUS'-tik) as an adjective may describe furniture or dwellings made of rough-hewn wood, or furnishings suitable to a farmhouse; or, when applied to a person, is an antonym of *urbane* – unsophisticated, boorish, lacking in social graces, uncultured. Noun: *rusticity* (rus-TIS'-i-ti). *Rustic* is also a noun designating a person with such characteristics.

   Urbane and *rustic*, when applied to people, are emotionally charged words. *Urbane* is complimentary, *rustic* derogatory.

Review of etymology

Write in the space provided an English word that uses each prefix, root, or suffix.

1.	*animus*	mind	_____
2.	*anima*	soul, spirit, life principle	_____
3.	*magnus*	large, great	_____
4.	*unus*	one	_____
5.	*verto, versus*	to turn	_____
6.	*stoa*	porch	_____
7.	*trepido*	to tremble	_____
8.	*scintilla*	a spark	_____
9.	*urbs*	city	_____
10.	*rus, ruris*	country, farmlands	_____

Can you match the words?

1. magnanimity	a. calmness, composure
2. urbanity	b. ability either to do many different things well, or to function successfully in many areas
3. unanimity	c. fearlessness; great courage
4. equanimity	d. unemotionality; bearing of pain, etc. without complaint
5. animus	e. big-heartedness; generosity
6. versatility	f. sparkling with wit, cleverness
7. stoicism	g. fear and trembling; alarm
8. intrepidity	h. complete agreement, all being of one mind
9. trepidation	i. sophistication, courtesy, etc.
10. scintillation	j. hostility, hatred

Key: 1-e, 2-i, 3-h, 4-a, 5-j, 6-b, 7-d, 8-c, 9-g, 10-f

Do you understand the words?

1. Is it easy to preserve one's *equanimity* under trying
   circumstances? YES NO
2. Do we bear *animus* towards our enemies? YES NO
3. Does a *pusillanimous* person often harbour thoughts
   of revenge? YES NO
4. Do we admire *versatility*? YES NO
5. Is *stoicism* a mark of an uninhibited personality? YES NO
6. Do cowards show *intrepidity* in the face of danger? YES NO
7. Do cowards often feel a certain amount of
   trepidation? YES NO
8. Is a *rustic* person suave and sophisticated? YES NO
9. Do dull people *scintillate*? YES NO
10. Is a village an *urban* community? YES NO

Key: 1-N, 2-Y, 3-Y, 4-Y, 5-N, 6-N, 7-Y, 8-N, 9-N, 10-N

Which is which?

Concave/convex
Concave refers to a surface that curves inward, and convex to a
surface that curves outwards. Remember by saying 'Concave – goes
in like a cave.'

Longitude/latitude
These are the words that geographers use to describe any particular
position on the Earth. Longitude describes the distance east or west
of the imaginary line that goes from the North Pole down through
Greenwich and across West Africa on its way to the South Pole.
Latitude is the distance north or south of the Equator.

Remember which is which by saying 'Latitude is FLATitude' –
it lies flat across the map.

Stalagmite/stalactite
The beautiful spiky shapes that form inside some caves are called
stalagmites if they grow upwards from the floor, and stalactites if
they grow down from the roof. Remember by saying 'Stalactite –
hold tite.'

TEST II
ANOTHER CHECK-UP ON YOUR PROGRESS

I Etymology

Root	Meaning	Example
1. *phanein*	_____	sycophant
2. *pater, patris*	_____	patricide
3. *onyma*	_____	synonym
4. *homos*	_____	homonym
5. *phone*	_____	homophone
6. *archein*	_____	matriarch
7. *mater, matris*	_____	matron
8. *caedo (-cide)*	_____	suicide
9. *homo*	_____	homicide
10. *uxor*	_____	uxorious
11. *sui-*	_____	suicide
12. *pyros*	_____	pyromania
13. *theos*	_____	atheist
14. *credo*	_____	credulous
15. *unus*	_____	unanimous
16. *trepido*	_____	intrepid
17. *scintilla*	_____	scintillate
18. *urbs*	_____	urbanity
19. *rus, ruris*	_____	rural, rustic
20. *gnosis*	_____	prognosis

II More etymology

Root	Meaning	Example
1. *mania*	_____	monomaniac
2. *anti-*	_____	antonym

3. *frater*	_____	fraternize
4. *soror*	_____	sorority
5. *claustra*	_____	claustrophobia
6. *akros*	_____	acrophobia
7. *hypo-*	_____	hypochondria
8. *dia-*	_____	diaphanous
9. *rex, regis*	_____	regal
10. *pono*	_____	impostor
11. *vivo*	_____	convivial
12. *verto, versus*	_____	versatile
13. *stoa*	_____	stoical
14. *ovum*	_____	ovary
15. *vita*	_____	vitality
16. *specto*	_____	spectator
17. *punctus*	_____	acupuncture
18. *acuo*	_____	acute
19. *per-*	_____	perspicuity
20. *retro-*	_____	retrospect

III Same or opposite?

1. atheistic – religious   S   O
2. convivial – unfriendly   S   O
3. ingenuous – naive   S   O
4. perspicacious – keen-minded   S   O
5. intrepid – fearful   S   O
6. tyro – virtuoso   S   O
7. megalomania – modesty   S   O
8. claustrophobia – agoraphobia   S   O
9. indefatigability – tirelessness   S   O
10. credulous – sceptical   S   O
11. martinet – slave-driver   S   O
12. sycophancy – slander   S   O
13. impostor – charlatan   S   O
14. antonym – synonym   S   O
15. homicide – murder   S   O
16. disingenuous – deceitful   S   O
17. vivacity – sluggishness   S   O
18. scintillating – witty   S   O
19. rustic – countrified   S   O
20. magnanimous – mean-minded   S   O

IV Matching

1. a masterly musician
2. sneers at tradition
3. fears being shut in
4. fatherly ruler
5. a dabbler
6. studies religion
7. a beginner
8. has imaginary ailments
9. compulsively starts fires
10. believes in one god

a. iconoclast
b. dilettante
c. theologian
d. pyromaniac
e. virtuoso
f. claustrophobe
g. tyro
h. monotheist
i. hypochondriac
j. patriarch

V More matching

1. love of parties
2. city sophistication
3. religious belief
4. sharp thinking
5. hostility
6. marriage
7. named after the father
8. pride in one's country
9. personal code of ethics
10. identifying a disease

a. creed
b. animus
c. urbanity
d. patriotism
e. patronymic
f. credo
g. conviviality
h. diagnosis
i. matrimony
j. acuity

VI Recall a word

1. inheritance from one's father   P _____
2. belief in many gods   P _____
3. unselfish; not revengeful   M _____
4. morbid fear of heights   A _____
5. the killing of one's brother   F _____
6. opposite in meaning (*adj.*)   A _____
7. to rob of life or vigour   D _____
8. inexperienced, unsophisticated   N _____
9. scrupulously careful in the observance of
   proper procedure   P _____
10. clear, understandable (of style or language)   P _____
11. wary, cautious, watchful   C _____
12. easily fooled   G _____

13. all of one mind (*adj.*)   U _____
14. uncomplaining in face of pain or misfortune S _____
15. killing of a race   G _____
16. crazily partisan for own country   C _____
17. an alcoholic   D _____
18. compulsion to steal   K _____
19. the emblems of the monarch   R _____
20. starting fires for financial gain   A _____

ANSWERS

Score 1 point for each correct answer.

I Etymology

1-to show, 2-father, 3-name, 4-same, 5-sound, 6-to rule, 7-mother, 8-to kill, 9-person, 10-wife, 11-oneself, 12-fire, 13-god, 14-to believe, 15-one, 16-to fear, 17-spark, 18-city, 19-country, farmland, 20-knowledge
Your score?

II More etymology

1-madness, 2-opposite, 3-brother, 4-sister, 5-enclosed space, 6-highest, 7-below, under, 8-through, 9-king, 10-to place, 11-to live, 12-to turn, 13-porch, 14-egg, 15-life, 16-to view, look at, 17-point, 18-sharp, 19-through, 20-backwards
Your score?

III Same or opposite?

1-O, 2-O, 3-S, 4-S, 5-O, 6-O, 7-O, 8-O, 9-S, 10-O, 11-S, 12-O, 13-S, 14-O, 15-S, 16-S, 17-O, 18-S, 19-S, 20-O
Your score?

IV Matching

1-e, 2-a, 3-f, 4-j, 5-b, 6-c, 7-g, 8-i, 9-d, 10-h
Your score?

V More matching

1-g, 2-c, 3-a, 4-j, 5-b, 6-i, 7-e, 8-d, 9-f, 10-h
Your score?

VI   Recall a word

1-patrimony,   2-polytheism,   3-magnanimous,   4-acrophobia,
5-fratricide,   6-antonym,   7-devitalize,   8-naive,   9-punctilious,
10-perspicuous,   11-circumspect,   12-gullible,   13-unanimous,
14-stoical,   15-genocide,   16-chauvinistic,   17-dipsomaniac,
18-kleptomania, 19-regalia, 20-arson
Your score?

Now add up your score over the whole test. The maximum possible
score is 100 points.

90–100	Masterly work; you have a talent for words.
80–89	Good work; you are making very satisfactory progress.
60–79	Average work; could you improve your study technique?
40–59	Not up to standard; work harder.
20–39	Poor; you need to revise before going on.
0–19	Why are you doing so badly?

The thrill of recognition

As time goes on and you notice more and more of the words you
have studied whenever you read, or whenever you listen to lectures,
the radio, or TV, the thrill of recognition plus the immediate
comprehension of complex ideas will provide a dividend of in-
calculable value.

You will hear these words in conversation, and you will begin to
use them yourself, unselfconsciously, whenever something you
want to say is best expressed by one of the words that exactly
verbalizes your thinking. Another priceless dividend!

*So keep on! You are involved in a dividend-paying activity that
will eventually make you intellectually rich.*

CHAPTER 6
THE PEOPLE YOU MEET

Every human being is, in one way or another, unique. Let us examine ten personality types (one of which might by chance be your very own) that result from the way culture, growth, family background, and environment interact with heredity.

SESSION 23 – TEN CHARACTERS IN SEARCH OF AN AUTHOR

1.　Me first

His attitude to life is simple – every decision he makes is based on the answer to one question: 'What is in it for me?' If his selfishness hurts other people, that is too bad.

　　　An *egoist*

2.　The height of conceit

'Have you heard about all the money I'm making? Did I tell you about my latest amorous conquest?' She is boastful to the point of being obnoxious. She has only one string to her conversational bow, namely, *herself*: what *she* has done, how good *she* is, how *she* would solve the problems of the world, etc.

　　　An *egotist*

3.　Let me help you

You have discovered the secret of true happiness – concerning yourself with the welfare of others. Never mind your own interests, how's the next fellow getting along?

　　　An *altruist*

4.　Leave me alone

You minutely examine your every thought and action. Futile questions like 'How do I look?', and 'Maybe I shouldn't have said that?' are your constant nagging companions. You may be shy and quiet, and you prefer solitude or at most the company of one person to a crowd. You probably have an aptitude for creative work.

An *introvert*

5. Let's do it together

You can always become interested – sincerely, vitally interested – in other people's problems. You're the life of the party, because you never inhibit yourself with doubts about dignity or propriety. You love to be with people – lots of people. Your thoughts and interests are turned outwards.

An *extrovert*

6. Never extreme

You have both introverted and extroverted tendencies – at different times and on different occasions. Your interests are turned, in about equal proportions, both inwards and outwards. Indeed, you're quite normal – in the sense that your personality is like that of most people.

An *ambivert*

7. People are no damn good

Cynical, embittered, suspicious, he hates everyone. The perfectibility of the human race? 'Nonsense! No way!' The stupidity, the meanness, and the crookedness of most mortals – that is his favourite theme.

A *misanthrope*

8. Women are no damn good

Sometime in your dim past, you were crossed, scorned, or deeply wounded by a woman (a mother, or mother figure, perhaps?). So now you have a carefully constructed defence against further hurt – you hate *all* women.

A *misogynist*

9. Foreigners are no damn good

This person has an irrational hatred and fear of anyone who comes from a different ethnic group. Ignoring the benefits to the local community and the country of having a rich cultural mix, he campaigns for 'Foreigners go home!'.

A *xenophobe*

10. The better way

Self-denial, austerity, lonely contemplation – these are the characteristics of the good life, so she claims. The simplest food and the least amount of it that will keep body and soul together, combined with abstinence from fleshly, earthly pleasures, will eventually lead to spiritual perfection – that is her philosophy.

An *ascetic*

Can you match the words?

1. egoist	a. turns thoughts inwards
2. egotist	b. hates foreigners
3. altruist	c. talks about accomplishments
4. introvert	d. hates people
5. extrovert	e. does not pursue pleasures of the flesh
6. ambivert	f. is interested in the welfare of others
7. misanthrope	g. believes in self-advancement
8. misogynist	h. turns thoughts both inwards and outwards
9. xenophobe	i. hates women
10. ascetic	j. turns thoughts outwards

Key: 1-g, 2-c, 3-f, 4-a, 5-j, 6-h, 7-d, 8-i, 9-b, 10-e

Do you understand the words?

1. Is an *egoist* selfish?   YES NO
2. Is modesty one of the characteristics of the *egotist*?   YES NO
3. Is an *altruist* selfish?   YES NO
4. Does an *introvert* pay much attention to himself?   YES NO
5. Does an *extrovert* prefer solitude to companionship? YES NO
6. Are most normal people *ambiverts*?   YES NO
7. Does a *misanthrope* like people?   YES NO
8. Does a *misogynist* enjoy the company of women?   YES NO
9. Is a *xenophobe* afraid of foreigners?   YES NO
10. Does an *ascetic* lead a life of luxury?   YES NO

Key: 1-Y, 2-N, 3-N, 4-Y, 5-N, 6-Y, 7-N, 8-N, 9-Y, 10-N

SESSION 24 – ME FIRST

1. The ego

Egoist (E'-gō-ist or EE'-gō-ist) and *egotist* (E'-gō-tist or EE'-gō-tist) are built on the same Latin root – the pronoun *ego*, meaning *I*. *I* is the greatest concern in the *egoist*'s mind, the most overused word in the *egotist*'s vocabulary. (Keep the words differentiated in your own mind by thinking of the *t* in *talk*, and the additional *t* in *egotist*.)

If you are an *egocentric* (ee'-gō-SEN'-trik or e'-gō-SEN'-trik), you consider yourself the *centre* of the universe – you are an extreme form of the *egoist*. And if you are an *egomaniac* (ee'-gō-MAY'-ni-ak or e'-gō-MAY'-ni-ak), you carry *egoism* to such an extreme that it has become a morbid obsession, a *mania*.

2. Others

In Latin, the word for *other* is *alter*, and a number of valuable English words are built on this root.

Altruism (AL'-trōō-iz-əm), the philosophy practised by *altruists*, comes from one of the variant spellings of Latin *alter*, other. *Altruistic* (al-trōō-IS'-tik) actions look towards the benefit of *others*. If you *alternate* (AWL'-tə-nayt'), you skip one and take the *other*, so to speak, as when you play golf on *alternate* (awl-TƏR'-nət) Saturdays. An *alteration* (awl'-tə-RAY'-shən) is of course a change – a making into something *other*.

An *altercation* (awl'-tə-KAY'-shən) is a verbal dispute, arising when one person has *other* ideas. *Altercation* is stronger than *quarrel* or *dispute*; you have *altercations* over pretty important issues, and you get quite excited.

Alter ego (AWL'-tə-EE'-gō), which combines *alter*, other, with *ego*, I, self, generally refers to someone with whom you are so close that you are almost mirror images of each other. Any such friend is your *other I*, your *other self*, your *alter ego*.

Can you match the words?

1. ego	a. one who is excessively fixated on his own desires, needs, etc.
2. egocentric	b. to change
3. altruism	c. argument

4. alter ego — d. one's concept of oneself
5. to alternate — e. to take one, skip one, etc.
6. egomaniacal — f. philosophy of putting another's welfare above one's own
7. to alter — g. one who talks about themself
8. altercation — h. a choice
9. alternative — i. morbidly obsessed with oneself
10. egotist — j. one's other self

Key: 1-d, 2-a, 3-f, 4-j, 5-e, 6-i, 7-b, 8-c, 9-h, 10-g

Do you understand the words?

1. Are *altruistic* tendencies common to egoists? YES NO
2. Does an *alternative* allow you some freedom of choice? YES NO
3. Is an *alternate* plan necessarily inferior? YES NO
4. Are *egomaniacal* tendencies a sign of maturity? YES NO
5. Is *altruism* a characteristic of selfish people? YES NO
6. Are *egocentric* people easy to get along with? YES NO
7. Does *alteration* imply keeping things the same? YES NO
8. Does an *egomaniac* have a normal personality? YES NO
9. Is rejection usually a blow to one's *ego*? YES NO
10. Do excitable people often engage in *altercations*? YES NO

Key: 1-N, 2-Y, 3-N, 4-N, 5-N, 6-N, 7-N, 8-N, 9-Y, 10-Y

SESSION 25 – TURN, TURN, TURN

1. Inside, outside

Introvert (IN'-trə-vərt), *extrovert* (EKS'-trə-vərt) and *ambivert* (AM'-bi-vərt) are built on the Latin verb *verto*, to turn. If your thoughts are constantly turned inwards (*intro-*), you are an *introvert*; outwards (*extra-*), an extrovert; and in both directions (*ambi-*), an *ambivert*.

The prefix *ambi-*, both, is also found in *ambidextrous* (am'-bi-DEKS'-trəs), *able to use both hands with equal skill.* The noun is *ambidexterity* (am'-bi-deks-TER'-ə-ti). *Dexterous* (DEKS'-trəs) means *skilful*, the noun *dexterity* (deks-TER'-ə-ti) is *skill*. *Dexter* is actually the Latin word for *right hand* – in the *ambidextrous* person, both hands are '*right*' hands. (Spelling caution: Note that the letter

following the *t-* in *ambidextrous* is *-r*, but that in *dexterous* the next
letter is *-e.)*

The Latin for *left* is *sinister*. Sinister (SIN'-i-stə), in English,
means *threatening, evil,* or *dangerous,* a commentary on our early
suspiciousness of left-handed persons. The French word for *left* is
gauche, and when we took this word over into English we invested it
with an uncomplimentary meaning. Call someone *gauche* (GŌSH)
and you imply clumsiness, generally social rather than physical.
A *gauche* remark is tactless; *gaucherie* (GŌ'-shə-ri) is a clumsy,
tactless, embarrassing way of saying things or of handling situations.

And the French word for *right* is *droit,* which we have used in
building our English word *adroit* (ə-DROYT'). Needless to say,
adroit, like *dexterous,* means *skilful,* but especially in the exercise of
the mental facilities. Like *gauche, adroit,* or its noun *adroitness,* usually
is used figuratively. The *adroit* person is quick-witted, can handle
situations ingeniously. *Adroitness* is the antonym of *gaucherie.*

2. Love, hate, and marriage

Misanthrope (MIZ'-ən-thrōp') and *misogynist* (mis-OJ'-ə-nist) are
built on the Greek root *misein,* to hate. The *misanthrope* hates mankind
(Greek *anthropos,* mankind), the *misogynist* hates women (Greek *gyne,*
woman).

Anthropos, mankind, is also found in *anthropology* (an'-thrə-POL'-ə-ji),
the study of the human race; and in *philanthropist* (fi-LAN'-thrə-pist), one
who loves mankind and shows such love by making financial contributions
to charity or by actively helping those in need.

The root *gyne,* woman, is also found in *gynaecologist* (gīna-ə-KOL'-ə-
jist), a doctor specializing in women's health. *Polygyny* (po-LIJ'-ə-ni)
combines this root with *poly,* many, to mean many women – or rather
many wives.

More usually we speak of *polygamy* (po-LIG'-ə-mi), meaning a system
of marriage with multiple spouses (usually wives); the root is Greek
gamos, marriage. We find this root again in *bigamy* (BIG'-ə-mi), having
two spouses (prefix *bi-,* two), and in *monogamy* (mo-NOG'-ə-mi), having
only one marriage (at a time) (prefix *mono-,* one). What if a woman has
two or more husbands? That custom is called *polyandry* (pol-i-AN'-dri),
from *poly* plus Greek *aner, andros,* man, husband.

Xenophobe (ZEN'-ə-fōb) combines the Greek *phobos,* fear, with
another Greek root, *xenos.* In ancient Greece this meant a stranger,
but also, just as importantly, a guest. In English, we have the meaning
of a stranger who is *un*welcome. A *xenophobe* is a person who hates and

fears strangers, particularly foreigners, and particularly ethnically different foreigners; the noun is *xenophobia* (zen'-ō-FŌB'-iə). You find a synonym in *racism* (a less usual word is *racialism*).

3. Living alone and liking it

Ascetic (ə-SET'-ik) is from the Greek word *asketes*, monk or hermit. Hence, that person is an *ascetic* who leads an existence, voluntarily of course, that compares in austerity and simplicity with the life of a monk. The practice is *asceticism* (ə-SET'-i-siz-əm), the adjective *ascetic*.

Teaser questions for the amateur etymologist – 6

1. If a *xenophobe* is afraid of foreigners, what is a *gynophobe* afraid of?
2. The Greek word for a dog is *cuon, cynos*. So what is the word for a person who is afraid of dogs?
3. The Greek word *morph* meaning shape can be used as a suffix to give words meaning *in the shape of*; for example, *anthropomorph*, something in the shape of a human being (as the Greek gods sometimes chose to be when they went out for fun). What shape might a person have if they were a *gynandromorph*?
4. The Latin word *lingua* for tongue or language has come down to us in several words. If someone who can speak two languages equally well is called *bilingual*, what about someone who can only speak one language?
5. *Sophia* is the Greek name for skill, learning, wisdom (and therefore a good name for a girl). Give the etymology of *philosophy*.

(*Answers in Chapter 11*)

Review of etymology

Write in the space provided an English word that uses each prefix, root, or suffix.

1. *ego*	self, I	_____
2. *alter*	other	_____
3. *ambi-*	both	_____
4. *misein*	hate	_____
5. *anthropos*	mankind	_____

6. *gyne*	woman	_____
7. *gamos*	marriage	_____
8. *dexter*	right hand	_____
9. *mono-*	one	_____
10. *bi-*	two	_____

Can you match the words?

1. anthropology	a. system of only one marriage
2. gynaecology	b. ability to use either hand
3. monogamy	c. clumsiness in social situations
4. xenophobia	d. study of humanity
5. gaucherie	e. study of women's ailments
6. introvert	f. devotion to a lonely and austere life
7. asceticism	g. skill, cleverness
8. philanthropy	h. a person whose thoughts turn inwards
9. adroitness	i. love of mankind
10. ambidexterity	j. hatred of foreigners

Key: 1-d, 2-e, 3-a, 4-j, 5-c, 6-h, 7-f, 8-i, 9-g, 10-b

Do you understand the words?

1. Does a *xenophobe* enjoy foreign travel?   YES NO
2. Is a surgeon likely to be *dexterous*?   YES NO
3. Is *gaucherie* a social asset?   YES NO
4. Is an *adroit* speaker likely to be a successful lawyer? YES NO
5. Is a student of *anthropology* interested in the Third
   World?   YES NO
6. Does a *gynaecologist* have more male than female
   patients?   YES NO
7. Is *monogamy* the custom in Western countries?   YES NO
8. Is a *philanthropist* generally altruistic?   YES NO
9. Are bachelors necessarily *misogynous*?   YES NO
10. Is *asceticism* compatible with the pursuit of
    pleasure?   YES NO

Key: 1-N, 2-Y, 3-N, 4-Y, 5-Y, 6-N, 7-Y, 8-Y, 9-N, 10-N

Stick to your time schedule!

Funny thing about time. Apart from the fact that we all, rich or poor, sick or well, have the same amount of time, exactly twenty-four hours every day, it is also true that we can always find time for the things we enjoy doing.

If you have enjoyed learning new words, accepting new challenges, gaining new understanding and discovering the thrill of accomplishment, then make sure to stay with the time schedule you have set yourself.

CHAPTER 7
THE GOOD, THE BAD, AND THE UGLY

In this chapter we will look at some more words to describe people and the way they behave. The central theme is the idea of 'fullness' – you can be full of compliance and servility; full of complaints; full of snobbery; full of noise; full of drink; full of sorrows; and many more.

SESSION 26 – TEN USEFUL WORDS ENDING IN -OUS

1. Compliance

The Latin root *sequor* means *to follow*. People in certain jobs – waiters, clerks, and domestic servants, for example – are forced, often contrary to their natural temperaments, to act in an excessively subservient and humble manner. They must follow the lead of their customers or employers, bending their own wills to the desires of those they serve. They are, etymologically, *full of following after*, or –

obsequious

2. Complaints

The Latin root *queror* means *to complain* – and anyone full of complaints, constantly nagging, harping, fretful, petulant, whining, never satisfied, may accordingly be called –

querulous

3. Snobbery

The Latin root *cilium* means *eyelid*; *super* means *above*; and above the eyelid, as anyone can plainly see, is the eyebrow. Now there are certain obnoxious people who go around raising their eyebrows in contempt and disdain at ordinary mortals like you and me. Such contemptuous, sneering, overbearingly conceited people are called –

supercilious

4. Noise

The Latin root *strepo* means *to make a noise*. Anyone who is unruly, boisterous, resistant to authority, unmanageable – and in a noisy, troublesome manner – is

obstreperous

5. Moneyless

The Latin root *pecus* means *cattle* – and at one time in human history a person's wealth was measured not by stocks and shares but by stocks of domestic animals. Someone who had pots of *pecus*, then, was rich – someone without *pecus* was out of money, broke. And so today we call someone who is habitually without funds, who seems generally to be full of a complete lack of money –

impecunious

6. Horses

The French word *cheval* means *horse*; and in medieval times only gentlemen and knights rode on horses – common people walked. Traditionally (but not necessarily in actual fact) knights were courteous to women and self-sacrifing when their own interests came in conflict with those of the fair sex. Hence we call a modern man who has a knightly attitude to women –

chivalrous

7. No harm done

The Latin root *noceo* means *to injure*; someone who need cause you no fear, so harmless is that person, so unable to interfere, so unlikely to get you into trouble, is called –

innocuous

8. alcoholic

The Latin root *bibo* means *to drink*; and one who likes to tipple beyond the point of sobriety, who has an overfondness for drinks with a pronounced alcoholic content, is called, usually humorously –

bibulous

9. Like death itself

The Latin root *cado* means *to fall* – one's final fall is of course always in death, and so someone who looks like a corpse (figuratively speaking), who is pale, gaunt, thin, haggard, with sunken eyes and wasted limbs, in other words the extreme opposite of the picture of glowing health, is called –

cadaverous

10. Pain and misery

The Latin root *doleo* means to *suffer* or *grieve* – one who is mournful and sad, whose melancholy comes from physical pain or mental distress, who seems to be suffering or grieving, is called –

dolorous

Review of etymology

Write in the space provided an English word that uses each prefix, root, or suffix.

1. *sequor*	to follow	_____
2. *queror*	to complain	_____
3. *cilium*	eyelid	_____
4. *strepo*	to make a noise	_____
5. *pecus*	cattle	_____
6. *-ary*	adjective suffix	_____
7. *im- (in-)*	negative prefix	_____
8. *cheval*	horse	_____
9. *bibo*	to drink	_____
10. *cado*	to fall	_____

Can you match the words?

1. obsequious	a. snobbish
2. querulous	b. harmless
3. supercilious	c. gaunt
4. obstreperous	d. short of funds
5. impecunious	e. ingratiatingly polite
6. chivalrous	f. sorrowful
7. innocuous	g. addicted to drink
8. bibulous	h. courteous to women
9. cadaverous	i. complaining
10. dolorous	j. unmanageable

Key: 1-e, 2-i, 3-a, 4-j, 5-d, 6-h, 7-b, 8-g, 9-c, 10-f

Do you understand the words?

1. Is a *bibulous* character a teetotaller?	YES	NO
2. Are *querulous* people satisfied?	YES	NO
3. Are *supercilious* people usually popular?	YES	NO
4. Are students generally *impecunious*?	YES	NO
5. Do some women like *chivalrous* men?	YES	NO
6. Are *innocuous* people dangerous?	YES	NO
7. Do *obsequious* people usually command our respect?	YES	NO
8. Is a *cadaverous*-looking individual the picture of health?	YES	NO
9. Is a *dolorous* attitude characteristic of gregarious people?	YES	NO
10. Is an *obstreperous* puppy hard to train?	YES	NO

Key: 1-N, 2-N, 3-N, 4-Y, 5-Y, 6-N, 7-N, 8-N, 9-N, 10-Y

SESSION 27 – VARIOUS GLOOMY WORDS

1.   An *obsequious* (əb-SEEK'-wi-əs) person is servile and fawning. The same Latin root, *sequor*, to follow, occurs in many English words.

1. *obsequies* – At a funeral, the mourners *follow after* the corpse. Hence, *obsequies* are the burial ceremonies, the funeral rites.

2. *sequel* – A *sequel* may be a literary work, such as a novel or a film, that *follows* another, continuing the same subject, dealing with the same people or village, etc. or it may be an occurrence that grows out of or *follows* another.

3. *sequence* – In order, one item *following* another, as in, 'The *sequence* of events of the next few days left him breathless.'

4. *subsequent* – A *subsequent* letter, paragraph, time, etc. is one that *follows* another.

Any other word containing the root *sequ-* is likely to have some relationship to the idea of *following*.

2. The Latin root *pecus* meaning *cattle* gives us *impecunious* (im-pə-KYōo-ni-əs). We also find it in *pecuniary* – pertaining to money, as in a *pecuniary* consideration, *pecuniary* affairs, etc. In law, *pecuniary advantage* has the meaning of financial gain dishonestly come by, and is a criminal offence.

3. *Cheval*, French for horse, comes from Latin *caballus*, an inferior horse. *Caballus* is found in English words in the spelling *caval-*.

    1. *cavalcade* – A procession of persons on horseback, as in a parade. The relatively new word *motorcade*, a procession in motor vehicles, was formed by analogy.

    2. *cavalier* – As a noun, a *cavalier* was once a mounted soldier. As an adjective, *cavalier* describes actions and attitudes that are haughty, unmindful of others' feelings, and offhand, such attributes often being associated with people in power (the military being one of the powers-that-be). Thus, 'After the *cavalier* treatment I received, I never wished to return', signifying that I was pretty much made to feel unimportant and inferior.

    3. *cavalry* – The mounted, or 'horsed' part of an army.

    4. *chivalry* – Noun form of *chivalrous*. Can you write the alternate noun form ending in *-ness*?

    5. *chivalric* – Less commonly used adjectival form, identical in meaning to *chivalrous*.

Another Latin root for *horse*, as you know, is *equus*, found in words we have already discussed, such as *equestrian* – a horseman, and *equine* – horselike. Another one is *equerry* (e-KWE'-ri), an officer in the royal household, originally responsible for the horses.

4. The Latin root *noceo* means to *injure*; from it comes *innocuous* (i-NOK'-yoo-əs), harmless. Related words include (1) *innocent* – not guilty of crime or injury; and, (2) *noxious* – harmful, poisonous; unwholesome.

Do not confuse *innocuous* with *inoculate* (to give an injection producing immunity), which is based on *in-* plus *oculus*, eye (see Chapter 8).

5. The Latin word *cado*, meaning to *fall*, is the root of *cadaver* – a corpse, literally, especially one used for surgical dissection. From that comes *cadaverous* (kə-DAV'-ər-əs), looking like a corpse.

Another derivative is *decadent* – etymologically, *falling down* (*de-* is a prefix one meaning of which is *down*, as in *descend*, climb down; *decline*, turn down, etc.). If something is in a *decadent* state, it is deteriorating, becoming corrupt or self-indulgent. *Decadence* is a state of decay. Generally *decadent* and *decadence* are used figuratively – they refer not to actual physical decay (as of a dead body), but to moral or spiritual decay, or a decline in artistic standards.

6. The Latin word *doleo*, to suffer, has a related noun, *dolor*, grief, sorrow. We are familiar with it as it occurs in the girl's name Dolores (actually derived from Spanish). Other related words are:

1. *dolorous* – causing grief or sorrow.

2. *doleful* – a word referring somewhat humorously to exaggerated dismalness, sadness, or dreariness; 'a basset hound has a doleful expression'.

3. *condole* – etymologically, to suffer or grieve with (Latin *con-*, with, together). The noun *condolence* is much more frequently heard than the verb, as in, 'Let me offer you my *condolences*', usually said to someone mourning the death of a friend or relative.

Even though it is undoubtedly a sorrowful experience to be *on the dole*, that word is unrelated. It comes from an Anglo-Saxon word *dal*, meaning a *share*.

Can you match the words?

1. obsequies		a. proper order
2. sequence		b. corpse
3. pecuniary		c. procession of mounted riders
4. noxious		d. pertaining to money
5. doleful		e. funeral rites
6. cavalcade		f. exaggeratedly sorrowful
7. equine		g. horselike
8. cadaver		h. spiritual or artistic decline
9. decadence		i. poisonous, harmful
10. condolence		j. expression of sympathy

Key: 1-e, 2-a, 3-d, 4-i, 5-f, 6-c, 7-g, 8-b, 9-h, 10-j

Do you understand the words?

1. Are speeches usually made during *obsequies*? YES NO
2. Is *Rocky II* a *sequel* to the film *Rocky*? YES NO
3. Is a banker an expert in *pecuniary* matters? YES NO
4. Is arsenic a *noxious* chemical? YES NO
5. Does a *cavalier* attitude show a spirit of humility? YES NO
6. Does an *equestrian* ride a bicycle? YES NO
7. Do humans possess many *equine* characteristics? YES NO
8. Is an iconoclast likely to consider religion a *decadent* institution? YES NO

9. Is *chivalry* dead?   YES NO
10. Are *condolences* appropriate at a
    wedding ceremony?   YES NO

Key: 1-Y, 2-Y, 3-Y, 4-Y, 5-N, 6-N, 7-N, 8-Y, 9-N (or Y, depending
on your point of view), 10-N

SESSION 28 – TEN MORE USEFUL WORDS

1. For want of funds

There are people who are forced (through no fault of their own) to
pursue an existence not only devoid of such luxuries as television sets,
electric orange-juice squeezers, Jacuzzis, etc., but lacking also in many
of the pure necessities of living – sufficient food, heated homes, hot
water, vermin-free surroundings, decent clothing, etc.

   Such people live:

in penury

2. At least watch it

If no one loves you, and if you can find no one on whom to lavish your
love, you may perhaps satisfy your emotional longings and needs by
getting your feelings secondhand – through reading love stories, going
to the movies, watching soap operas, etc.

   These are:

vicarious feelings

3. Truth to tell

Some people are naturally incapable of a lie. Even in circumstances
where it might be more comfortable for all concerned if they covered
up a bit, they will tell the truth, the whole truth and nothing but the
truth.

   They are:

veracious

4. How not to call a spade . . .

Words are only *symbols* of things – they are not the things themselves.
But many people identify the word and the thing so closely that they
fear to use certain words that symbolize things that are unpleasant to
them. These people prefer circumlocutions – words that 'talk around'

an idea or that imply something but don't come right out and say so directly. For example:

Word	Circumlocution
die	depart this life; pass away
tell a lie	be economical with the truth
buttocks	derrière; rear end; behind; sit-upon; backside; posterior
urinate (women)	spend a penny; wash your hands
drunk	tired and emotional

The left-hand column is the direct, non-pussyfooting word. The right-hand column is made up of:

euphemisms

5. Small talk

Never bogged down in euphemisms, always ready to talk, never at a loss for words, some people are unfailingly:

fluent

6. Everything but give milk

You've seen a cow contentedly munching the cud. Nothing seems capable of disturbing this animal – and the animal seems to want nothing more out of life than to lead a simple, vegetable existence.

Some people are like a cow – calm, patient, placid. They are:

bovine

7. Good old days

Do you sometimes experience a keen, almost physical, longing for associations or places of the past? When you are away from home and friends and family, do pleasant remembrances crowd in on your mind to the point where your present loneliness becomes almost unbearable, and you actually feel a little sick?

This common feeling is called:

nostalgia

8. Sounds that grate

Some sounds are so harsh, grating, and discordant that they offend the ear. They lack all sweetness, harmony, pleasantness. Traffic noises, a flock of seagulls . . .

Such blaring, ear-splitting sounds are called:

cacophonous

9. Eating habits

Lions, tigers, wolves, and some other mammals subsist entirely on flesh. So also do spiders which trap and eat insects.

These creatures are:

carnivorous

10. Private and public

There are certain things most of us do in private, like taking a bath. Some people like to engage in other activities in complete privacy – eating, reading, watching TV, for example. The point is that, while these activities may be conducted in privacy, there is never a reason for keeping them secret.

But there are other activities that are not only kept private, but are well-shrouded in secrecy and concealed from public knowledge. These activities are unethical, illegal, or unsafe – like having an affair with your best friend's husband, bribing public officials, hiring a hit-man, etc.

Such arrangements, activities, or meetings are called:

clandestine

Can you match the words?

1.	penury	a.	always honest
2.	vicarious	b.	talkative
3.	fluent	c.	homesickness
4.	euphemism	d.	meat-eating
5.	veracious	e.	circumlocution
6.	bovine	f.	harsh noise
7.	nostalgia	g.	poverty
8.	cacophony	h.	secret
9.	carnivorous	i.	placid; stolid; cowlike
10.	clandestine	j.	experienced at one remove

Key: 1-g, 2-j, 3-b, 4-e, 5-a, 6-i, 7-c, 8-f, 9-d, 10-h

Do you understand the words?

1. Do wealthy people normally live in *penury*?   YES NO
2. Is a *vicarious* thrill one that comes from direct participation?   YES NO

3. Do *veracious* people tell lies?   YES NO
4. Is a *euphemism* likely to be used by a down-to-earth person?   YES NO
5. Are *bovine* people highly-strung and nervous?   YES NO
6. Is a *fluent* person often stuck for the right word?   YES NO
7. Does one get a feeling of *nostalgia* for past times?   YES NO
8. Is *cacophony* pleasant and musical?   YES NO
9. Do *carnivorous* animals eat meat?   YES NO
10. Is a *clandestine* meeting conducted in secrecy?   YES NO

Key: 1-N, 2-N, 3-N, 4-N, 5-N, 6-N, 7-Y, 8-N, 9-Y, 10-Y

SESSION 29 – TRUTH AND LIKENESS

1. Money, and what it will buy

Penury (PEN'-yoo-ri), from Latin *penuria*, need, neediness, is dire, abject poverty, complete lack of financial resources. A close synonym of *penury*, and one of equal strength, is *destitution* (des-ti-TYOO-shən). *Destitute* (DES'-ti-ty$\overline{oo}$t) people do not even have the means for mere subsistence – as such, they are perhaps on the verge of starvation. A milder degree of poverty is indicated by the word *indigence* (IN'-di-jəns); indigent people are not absolutely penniless, merely living in reduced circumstances.

To turn now to the brighter side, having plenty of money is expressed by *affluence* (AF'-loo-əns). *Affluent* (AF'-loo-ənt) people, or those living in *affluent* circumstances, are more than comfortable. A much stronger term is *opulence* (OP'-yoo-ləns), which not only implies much greater wealth than *affluence*, but in addition suggests lavish expenditures and ostentatiously luxurious surroundings; more money than taste.

Affluent is a combination of the prefix *ad-*, to, towards (changing to *af-* before a root beginning with *f*), plus the Latin verb *fluo*, to flow – *affluence* is that delightful condition in which money keeps flowing to us. *Opulent* is from Latin *opulentus*, wealthy. No other English words derive from this root.

2. Doing and feeling

If you watch a furious athletic event, and *you* get tired, though the athletes expend all the energy – that's *vicarious* fatigue. If you watch a mother in a film or play suffer horribly at the death of her child, and *you* go through the same agony, that's *vicarious* torment.

The word comes from Latin *vicarius*, a deputy. And that's where the vicar comes in – technically, he is the deputy priest in place of the rector.

3. Nothing but the truth

Habitually honest people are *veracious* (və-RAY'-shəs); their quality of truthfulness is *veracity* (və-RAS'-i-ti). (Do not confuse these with voracious, voracity – see next Session!) The Latin root is *verus*, true. It also occurs in the English words to *aver* (ə-VER'), to assert that something is true; *verify*, to check the truth of something; and *verisimilitude* (ve'-ri-si-MIL'-i-tyo͞od), likeness to the truth. *Verus* is also the source of our *very*.

4. An exploration of various good things

A *euphemism* is a word or expression that has been substituted for another that is likely to offend – it is built on the Greek prefix *eu-*, good, the root *pheme*, voice, and the noun suffix *-ism*. (Etymologically, 'Something said in a good voice'.) Adjective: *euphemistic* (yo͞o'-fə-MIS'-tik).

Other English words constructed from the prefix *eu-*:

1. *euphony* (YO͞O'-fə-ni) – good sound; pleasant lilt or rhythm (*phone, sound*). Adjective: *euphonic* (yo͞o-FON'-ik) or *euphonious* (yo͞o-FŌ'-ni-əs).

2. *eulogy* (YO͞O'-lə-ji) – etymologically, 'good speech'; a formal speech of praise, usually delivered as a funeral oration. *Logos* here means *word* or *speech*, as it also does in *monologue, dialogue, epilogue*, and *prologue*; but *logos* more commonly means *science* or *study*. Adjective: *eulogistic* (yo͞o-lə-JIS'-tik); verb: *eulogize* (YO͞O'-lə-jīz').

3. *euphoria* (yo͞o-FAW'-ri-ə) – good feeling, a sense of mental buoyancy and physical well-being. Adjective: *euphoric* (yo͞o-FOR'-ik).

4. *euthanasia* (yo͞o'-thə-NAY'-zi-ə) – etymologically, 'good death'; method of painless death for people suffering from incurable diseases – not legal at the present time, but advocated by many people. The word derives from *eu-* plus Greek *thanatos*, death.

5. So to speak

A *fluent* person produces words in a flow – the Latin root is *fluo*, to flow, which we have already met in *affluent*. Other derivatives include *fluid, influence*, and *confluence* (a 'flowing together').

Our speakers' *fluency* (FLO͞O'-ən-si) will enable them to avoid the following two faults of expression.

A *cliché* (KLEE'-shay) is a pattern of words which was once new and fresh, but which now is so old and threadbare that only banal, unimaginative speakers and writers ever use it. Examples are: *fast and furious*; *unsung heroes*; *by leaps and bounds*; *conspicuous by its absence*; *green with envy*; etc. The most pointed insult to a person's way of talking is, 'You speak in *clichés*.'

A *platitude* is similar to a *cliché*, in that it is a dull, trite, hackneyed, unimaginative pattern of words – but, to add insult to injury (*cliché*), the speaker uses it as if he just made it up!

Platitude (PLAT'-i-tyōod) derives from Greek *platy*, broad or flat, plus the noun suffix -*tude*. Words like *plateau* (flat land), *plate* and *platter* (flat dishes), and *platypus* (flat foot) all derive from the same root as *platitude*, a flat statement, i.e., one that falls flat, despite the speaker's high hopes for it. The adjective is *platitudinous* (plat'-i-TYŌO'-di-nəs).

Review of etymology

Write in the space provided an English word that uses each prefix, root, or suffix.

1. *penuria*	need, neediness	_____
2. *ad-* (*af-*)	to, towards	_____
3. *fluo*	to flow	_____
4. *-ence*	noun suffix	_____
5. *eu-*	good	_____
6. *pheme*	voice	_____
7. *logos*	word, speech	_____
8. *-ize*	verb suffix	_____
9. *thanatos*	death	_____
10. *platy*	broad or flat	_____

Can you match the words?

1. fluent	a. mental well-being
2. destitute	b. smooth-talking
3. opulent	c. truthful
4. vicarious	d. hackneyed phrase
5. euphonic	e. ostentatiously wealthy
6. veracious	f. likeness to the truth
7. euphoria	g. pleasant-sounding

8. eulogize	h. in want
9. verisimilitude	i. secondhand
10. cliché	j. praise

Key: 1-b, 2-h, 3-e, 4-i, 5-g, 6-c, 7-a, 8-j, 9-f, 10-d

Do you understand the words?

1. Do *penurious* people satisfy their extravagant desires?	YES	NO
2. Can you engage in *vicarious* exploits by reading spy novels?	YES	NO
3. Is *indigence* a sign of wealth?	YES	NO
4. Is a *destitute* person likely to have to live in want?	YES	NO
5. Are *opulent* surroundings indicative of great wealth?	YES	NO
6. Do parents generally indulge in *euphemisms* in front of young children?	YES	NO
7. Is *euphoria* a feeling of malaise?	YES	NO
8. Is *euthanasia* practised on animals?	YES	NO
9. Is a *platitude* flat and dull?	YES	NO
10. Are the works of Beethoven considered *euphonious*?	YES	NO

Key: 1-N, 2-Y, 3-N, 4-Y, 5-Y, 6-Y, 7-N, 8-Y, 9-Y, 10-Y

SESSION 30 – Etymologically speaking

1. People are the craziest animals

Bovine (BŌ'-vīn), placid like a cow, is built on *bos, bovis*, the Latin word for *ox* or *cow*, plus the suffix *-ine*, like, similar to, or characteristic of. To call someone *bovine* is of course far from complimentary. Humans are sometimes compared to other animals, as in the following adjectives:

1. *leonine* (LEE'-ə-nīn') – like a lion in appearance or temperament (Latin *leo*, lion)

2. *canine* (KAY'-nīn') – like a dog; our canine teeth are similar to those of a dog (Latin *canis*, dog)

3. *feline* (FEE'-līn') – catlike (Latin *felis*, cat)

4. *porcine* (PAW'-sīn') – piglike (Latin *porcus*, pig; hence pork)

5. *equine* (E'-kwīn') – horselike; 'horsy' (Latin *equus*, horse; see Chapter 1 for more words)

All these words can also be nouns meaning a member of the species in question; thus 'All *felines* have whiskers.'

2. You can't go home again

Nostalgia (nos-TAL'-jə), built on two Greek roots, *nostos*, a return to home, and *algos*, pain (as in *neuralgia, cardialgia*, etc.) is a feeling you can't understand until you've experienced it. Your memory tends to store up the pleasant experiences of the past and when you are lonely or unhappy you may begin to relive these pleasant occurrences. It is then that you feel the emotional pain and longing that we call *nostalgia*.

Purists assert that it can only refer to longing for a *place*, because of the meaning of its Greek root, but in fact it is more often used about a past *time*, as in 'I can't help feeling *nostalgic* for the sixties.'

3. Soundings

Cacophony (ka-KOF'-ə-ni) is itself a harsh-sounding word – and is the only one that exactly describes the ear-offending noises you are likely to hear in man-made surroundings. It is built on the Greek roots *kakos*, bad, harsh, or ugly, and *phone*, sound. Adjective: *cacophonous* (kə-KOF'-ə-nəs).

Phone, sound, is found also in:
1. *telephone* – sound from afar (Greek *tele-*, far)
2. *euphony* – pleasant sound (Greek *eu-*, good)
3. *saxophone* – a musical instrument (hence *sound*) invented by Adolphe Sax
4. *xylophone* – a musical instrument; 'sounds through wood' (Greek *xylon*, wood)
5. *phonetics* (fə-NET'-iks) – the science of the sounds of language; the adjective is *phonetic* (fə-NET'-ik), the expert a *phonetician* (fō'-nə-TISH'-ən).

4. The flesh and all

Carnivorous combines *carnis*, flesh, and *voro*, to devour. A *carnivorous* (kah-NIV'-ə-rəs) animal, or *carnivore* (KAH'-ni-vaw'), is one whose main diet is meat.

Voro, to devour, is the origin of other words referring to eating habits:
1. *herbivorous* (hər-BIV'-ər-əs) – subsisting on vegetation, as do cows, deer, horses, etc. The animal is a *herbivore* (HəR'-bi-vaw). (Latin *herba*, herb.)
2. *omnivorous* (om-NIV'-ər-əs) – eating everything: meat, grains, grasses, fish, insects, and anything else digestible. Humans are

omnivores by nature; so, for example, are hedgehogs. *Omnivorous* (Latin *omnis*, all) refers not only to food: an *omnivorous* reader reads everything in great quantities (that is, devours *all* kinds of books).
3. *voracious* (və-RAY'-shəs) – *devouring*; hence, greedy or gluttonous; one may be a *voracious* eater, *voracious* reader, *voracious* in one's pursuit of money, etc. Think of the two noun forms of *loquacious*. Can you write two nouns derived from *voracious*?

5.   'Allness'

Latin *omnis*, all, is the origin of:
1. *omnipotent* (om-NIP'-ə-tənt) – all-powerful. This comes from the Latin *potens*, *potentis*, powerful, as in *potentate*, a powerful ruler; *impotent* (IM'-pə-tənt), powerless; *potent*, powerful; and *potential*, possessing power or ability not yet exercised. Can you write the noun form of *omnipotent*?
2. *omniscient* (om-NIS'-i-ənt) – all-knowing: hence, infinitely wise (Latin *sciens*, knowing).
3. *omnipresent* (om'-ni-PREZ'-ənt) – present in all places at once. A synonym of *omnipresent* is *ubiquitous* (yoo-BIK'-wi-təs), from Latin *ubique*, everywhere. '*Ubiquitous* laughter greeted the press secretary's remark', i.e., laughter was heard *everywhere* in the room.

6.   More flesh

Note how *carnis*, flesh, is the building block of:
1. *carnelian* (kah-NEEL'-yən) – a reddish gemstone, the colour of red *flesh*.
2. *carnival* (KAH'-ni-vəl) – originally the season of merrymaking just before Lent, when people took a last fling before saying '*Carne vale!*' 'Oh *flesh*, farewell!' (Latin *vale*, farewell, goodbye).
3. *carnal* (KAH'-nəl) – of the *flesh*, as in phrases like '*carnal* pleasures' or '*carnal* appetites'. The noun is *carnality* (kah-NAL'-i-ti).
4. *carnage* (KAH'-nij) – great destruction of life (that is, of human *flesh*), as in war or mass murders.
5. *reincarnation* (ree'-in-kah-NAY'-shən) – a rebirth or reappearance. Believers in *reincarnation* maintain that one's soul takes on new *flesh* after death. The verb is to *reincarnate* (ree'-IN'-kah-nayt), to bring (a soul) back in another bodily form.
6. *incarnate* (in-KAH'-nət) – in the *flesh*. If we use this adjective to call someone 'the devil *incarnate*', we mean that here is the devil in the *flesh*. The verb to *incarnate* (IN'-kah-nayt) is to embody, give bodily form to, or make real.

Teaser questions for the amateur etymologist – 7

1. The negative prefix *in-* plus *doleo*, to suffer, together form an adjective that etymologically should mean *not suffering*, but actually means *idle, lazy, disliking effort or work*. What is this word? What is the noun form?

2. In logic, a conclusion not based on the evidence is called a *non sequitur*; by extension the term is applied to any statement that appears to have no connection to what was said before. Knowing the root *sequor*, how would you define this term etymologically?

3. We have seen that the Latin root *verto, versus* means to turn. How do you explain the origin of (a) inversion; (b) subversion?

4. *Pre-* is a prefix that can mean before, or beyond. What does it mean in *prehistoric*?

5. Latin *super*, above or over, is used as a prefix in hundreds of English words. Can you work out a word starting with *super-* to fit each definition?

   (a) above others (in quality, position, etc.)
   (b) ghostly; above (or beyond) the natural
   (c) to oversee; to be in charge of

(*Answers in Chapter 11*)

---

7. Dark secrets

Clandestine comes from Latin *clam*, secretly, and implies secrecy or concealment in the working out of a plan that is dangerous or illegal. *Clandestine* is a stronger word than *surreptitious* (sur'-əp-TISH'-əs), which means *stealthy, sneaky, furtive*, generally because of fear of detection.

Review of etymology

Write in the space provided an English word that uses each prefix, root, or suffix.

1. *-ine*   like, similar to   _____
2. *algos*   pain   _____
3. *phone*   sound   _____
4. *carnis*   flesh   _____
5. *voro*   to devour   _____
6. *omnis*   all   _____
7. *potens, potentis* powerful   _____

8. *sciens*	knowing	_____
9. *ubique*	everywhere	_____
10. *re-*	again, back	_____

Can you match the words?

1. canine	a. found everywhere
2. feline	b. greedy, devouring
3. voracious	c. all-powerful
4. omnipotent	d. stealthy, clandestine
5. omniscient	e. all-knowing
6. surreptitious	f. catlike
7. nostalgic	g. harsh-sounding
8. cacophonous	h. eating everything
9. omnivorous	i. doglike
10. ubiquitous	j. homesick

Key: 1-i, 2-f, 3-b, 4-c, 5-e, 6-d, 7-j, 8-g, 9-h, 10-a

Do you understand the words?

1. *Porcine* appearance means wolflike appearance	YES NO
2. *Nostalgic* feelings refer to a longing for past experiences	YES NO
3. *Cacophonous* music is pleasant and sweet	YES NO
4. An elephant is a *carnivore*	YES NO
5. An *omnivorous* reader does very little reading	YES NO
6. True *omnipotence* is unattainable by human beings	YES NO
7. No one is *omniscient*	YES NO
8. *Carnelian* is a deep blue gemstone	YES NO
9. *Carnality* is much respected in a puritanical society	YES NO
10. A *surreptitious* glance is meant to be conspicuous	YES NO

Key: 1-N, 2-Y, 3-N, 4-N, 5-N, 6-Y, 7-Y, 8-N, 9-N, 10-N

TEST III
A FURTHER PROGRESS CHECK

I Etymology

Root	Meaning	Example
1. *fluo*	_____	affluent
2. *pheme*	_____	euphemism
3. *platy*	_____	platitude
4. *felis*	_____	feline
5. *nostos*	_____	nostalgia
6. *philos*	_____	philanthropy
7. *carnis*	_____	carnivorous
8. *voro*	_____	voracious
9. *omnis*	_____	omnivorous
10. *ubique*	_____	ubiquity
11. *doleo*	_____	dolorous
12. *porcus*	_____	porcine
13. *thanatos*	_____	euthanasia
14. *canis*	_____	canine
15. *algos*	_____	nostalgic
16. *logos*	_____	eulogy
17. *sciens, scientis*	_____	omniscient
18. *phone*	_____	euphonious
19. *penuria*	_____	penury
20. *gamos*	_____	monogamy

II More etymology

Root	Meaning	Example
1. *sequor, secutus*	_____	obsequious
2. *pecus*	_____	impecunious
3. *equus*	_____	equine

4. *caballus (caval-)*	_____	cavalier
5. *noceo*	_____	innocuous
6. *cilium*	_____	supercilious
7. *cado*	_____	cadaverous
8. *kakos*	_____	cacophony
9. *verus*	_____	verify
10. *eu-*	_____	euphoria
11. *ego*	_____	egotist
12. *xenos*	_____	xenophobia
13. *phobos*	_____	xenophobia
14. *intro-*	_____	introvert
15. *misein*	_____	misanthrope
16. *gyne*	_____	gynaecologist
17. *aner, andros*	_____	polyandry
18. *alter*	_____	alternate
19. *asketes*	_____	ascetic
20. *loquor, locutus*	_____	circumlocution

III Same or opposite?

1. penury – affluence	S	O
2. vicarious – secondhand	S	O
3. noxious – poisonous	S	O
4. carnivorous – vegetarian	S	O
5. cacophony – euphony	S	O
6. clandestine – surreptitious	S	O
7. parsimonious – extravagant	S	O
8. indigent – opulent	S	O
9. destitute – impecunious	S	O
10. euphemistic – indirect	S	O
11. ascetic – voluptuary	S	O
12. platitudinous – original	S	O
13. voracious – gluttonous	S	O
14. omniscient – ignorant	S	O
15. omnipresent – ubiquitous	S	O
16. extrovert – introvert	S	O
17. carnage – slaughter	S	O
18. adroit – dexterous	S	O
19. egoism – altruism	S	O
20. gauche – clumsy	S	O

IV Matching

1. vicarious	a. excessively polite or servile
2. cavalier (*adj.*)	b. gaunt, corpselike
3. egocentric	c. noisy, boisterous
4. obsequious	d. wealthy
5. querulous	e. high-handed
6. obstreperous	f. sad
7. innocuous	g. nagging, complaining
8. cadaverous	h. harmless
9. dolorous	i. second-hand
10. opulent	j. self-centred

V More matching

1. condolence	a. outgoing personality
2. decadent	b. harsh sound
3. altruistic	c. having many wives
4. extrovert	d. a return to life in a new form
5. surreptitious	e. eating everything
6. cacophony	f. expression of sympathy
7. reincarnation	g. cowlike; phlegmatic; stolid
8. omnivorous	h. morally deteriorating
9. polygamous	i. unselfish
10. bovine	j. stealthy; secret

VI Recall a word

1. lionlike	L _____
2. doglike	C _____
3. catlike	F _____
4. piglike	P _____
5. horselike	E _____
6. all-powerful	O _____
7. in the flesh	I _____
8. secret, shameful	C _____
9. meat-eating (*adj.*)	C _____
10. habitually truthful	V _____
11. speech of praise	E _____
12. a feeling of well-being	E _____
13. mercy death	E _____

14. talking in an effortless flow   F _____
15. a woman-hater   M_____
16. one whose character is neither inturned nor
    outgoing   A _____
17. study of the human race   A _____
18. relating to, pertaining to, or involving
    money (*adj.*)   P _____
19. harmless   I _____
20. snobbish; haughty   S _____

ANSWERS

Score 1 point for each correct answer.

I Etymology

1-to flow, 2-voice, 3-flat, broad, 4-cat, 5-a return (to home), 6-love, 7-flesh, 8-to devour, 9-all, 10-everywhere, 11-to suffer, grieve, 12-pig, 13-death, 14-dog, 15-pain, 16-word, speech, 17-knowing, 18-sound, 19-want, neediness, 20-marriage
Your score?

II More etymology

1-to follow, 2-cattle, 3-horse, 4-horse, 5-to injure, 6-eyelid, 7-to fall, 8-ugly, bad, 9-true, 10-good, well, 11-I, myself, 12-foreigner, stranger, 13-fear, 14-inwards, 15-to hate, 16-woman, 17-man, husband, 18-other, 19-monk, hermit, 20-to speak
Your score?

III Same or opposite?

1-O, 2-S, 3-S, 4-O, 5-O, 6-S, 7-O, 8-O, 9-S, 10-S, 11-O, 12-O, 13-S, 14-O, 15-S, 16-O, 17-S, 18-S, 19-O, 20-S
Your score?

IV Matching

1-i, 2-e, 3-j, 4-a, 5-g, 6-c, 7-h, 8-b, 9-f, 10-d
Your score?

V More matching

1-f, 2-h, 3-i, 4-a, 5-j, 6-b, 7-d, 8-e, 9-c, 10-g
Your score?

VI Recall a word

1-leonine, 2-canine, 3-feline, 4-porcine, 5-equine, 6-omnipotent, 7-incarnate, 8-clandestine, 9-carnivorous, 10-veracious, 11-eulogy, 12-euphoria, 13-euthanasia, 14-fluent, 15-misogynist, 16-ambivert, 17-anthropology, 18-pecuniary, 19-innocuous, 20-supercilious
Your score?

Now add up your score over the whole test. The maximum possible score is 100 points.

90–100	Masterly
80–89	Good
60–79	Average
40–59	Unsatisfactory
20–39	Poor
0–19	Surely not!

You are now nearly three-quarters of the way through the book. When you look back at your scores on this and the earlier two tests, do you find that you are improving?

Adder nuff?

Some English words, in their journey down the centuries, have become slightly muddled. In a few cases, words that should begin with *n* have lost their first letter because it has got turned into the *n* of *an*. Here's an example:

An *orange* should be a *norange*. It comes from Arabic *naranj*.

Others are *adder*, which is from an Anglo-Saxon word *naedre*, a snake, so it should be a *nadder*; and *apron*, from French *naperon*, a little cloth.

It can happen the other way round, too. A *newt* should really be an *ewt* (from Anglo-Saxon *efeta*, a newt)

CHAPTER 8
IS THERE A DOCTOR IN THE HOUSE?

In this chapter we discuss medical specialists – what they do, how they do it, what they are called.

SESSION 31 – TEN DIFFERENT SPECIALISTS

1. Women's health

This specialist treats the parts of a woman's body that are concerned with sex and having babies.

> A *gynaecologist*

2. A baby is born

This specialist delivers babies and takes care of the mother during and immediately after the period of her pregnancy.

> An *obstetrician*

3. Newborn babies and young children

This specialist limits his or her practice to youngsters, taking care of babies directly after birth, including intensive-care treatment for premature babies. He/she supervises the baby's diet and watches over its growth and development, giving the series of inoculations that has done so much to decrease infant mortality. He/she has extensive knowledge of the common infectious diseases of childhood, such as mumps, as well as the rare ones such as meningitis.

> A *paediatrician*

4. Skin clear?

You have heard the classic riddle: 'What is the best use for pigskin?' answer: 'To keep the pig together.' Human skin has a similar purpose: it is what keeps us all in one piece, and protects our insides from the outside world. And our outer covering is subject to diseases and infections of various kinds, running the gamut from harmless spots to fatal cancer. There is a specialist who treats all such skin diseases.

A *dermatologist*

5.   Looking well, seeing well

The doctor whose speciality is disorders of vision (myopia, astigmatism, cataracts, glaucoma, etc.) may prescribe glasses, administer drugs, or perform surgery.

An *ophthalmologist*

6.   A feeling in your bones

This specialist deals with the skeletal structure of the body, treating bone fractures, slipped discs, clubfoot, curvature of the spine, dislocations of the hip, etc., and may correct a condition either by surgery or by the use of braces or other appliances.

An *orthopaedist* or *orthopaedic surgeon*

7.   Does your heart go pitter-patter?

This specialist treats disorders of the heart and circulatory system, sometimes with drugs but increasingly with sophisticated surgical techniques.

A *cardiologist*

8.   In the blood

This doctor specializes in disorders of the blood, including leukaemia, which is a cancer of the bone-marrow (where blood components are formed).

A *haematologist*

9.   Nerves and brain

This physician specializes in the treatment of disorders of the brain, spinal cord, and the rest of the nervous system.

A *neurologist*

10.   Nerves and nervousness

This specialist attempts to alleviate mental and emotional disturbances by means of various techniques, sometimes drugs, but more often one-to-one or group psychotherapy.

A *psychiatrist*

Can you match the subject with the person?

1. mental or emotional disturbances	a. gynaecologist
2. nervous system	b. obstetrician
3. skin	c. paediatrician
4. infants	d. dermatologist
5. female reproductive organs	e. ophthalmologist
6. eyes	f. orthopaedist
7. heart	g. cardiologist
8. blood	h. neurologist
9. pregnancy, childbirth	i. haematologist
10. skeletal system	j. psychiatrist

Key: 1-j, 2-h, 3-d, 4-c, 5-a, 6-e, 7-g, 8-i, 9-b, 10-f

Do you understand the words?

1. Is a *gynaecologist* familiar with the female reproductive organs?   YES   NO
2. Does an *obstetrician* specialize in diseases of childhood?   YES   NO
3. Does a *paediatrician* deliver babies?   YES   NO
4. If you had a skin disease, would you visit a *dermatologist*?   YES   NO
5. If you had trouble with your vision, would you visit an *orthopaedist*?   YES   NO
6. Is an *ophthalmologist* an eye specialist?   YES   NO
7. Does a *cardiologist* treat bone fractures?   YES   NO
8. Is a *neurologist* a nerve specialist?   YES   NO
9. If you were nervous and constantly fearful for no apparent reasons, would a *psychiatrist* be the specialist to see?   YES   NO
10. Does a *haematologist* specialize in men's diseases?   YES   NO

Key: 1-Y, 2-N, 3-N, 4-Y, 5-N, 6-Y, 7-N, 8-Y, 9-Y, 10-N

SESSION 32 – WOMEN AND CHILDREN FIRST

1. Doctors for women

The word *gynaecologist* (gīn'-ə-KOL'-ə-jist) is built on Greek *gyne*, woman, plus *logy*, science, which comes from the Greek *logos*, meaning word; etymologically, *gynaecology* is the science of women. Adjective: *gynaecological* (gīn'-ə-kə-LOJ'-i-kəl).

Obstetrician (ob'-stə-TRISH'-ən) derives from Latin *obstetrix*, midwife, which in turn has its source in a Latin verb meaning *to stand* – midwives stand in front of the woman in labour to deliver the baby.

The medical speciality dealing with childbirth is *obstetrics* (ob-STET'-riks). Adjective: *obstetric* (ob-STET'-rik) or *obstetrical* (ob-STET'-ri-kəl).

The suffix -*ician*, as in *obstetrician, physician, musician, magician, electrician*, etc., means *expert*.

2. Children

Paediatrician (pee'-di-ə-TRISH'-ən) is a combination of Greek *paidos*, child; *iatreia*, medical healing; and -*ician*, expert. *Paediatrics* (pee-di-AT'-riks), then, is the medical healing of a child. Adjective: *paediatric* (pee-di-AT'-rik).

Pedagogy (PED'-ə-go'-ji), which loses the 'a' but still combines *paidos* with *agogos*, leading, is, etymologically, *the leading of children*. And to what do you lead them? To learning, to development, to maturity. Hence, *pedagogy*, which by derivation means *the leading of a child*, refers actually to the principles and methods of teaching. Adjective: *pedagogic* (ped'-ə-GOJ'-ik) or *pedagogical* (ped'-ə-GOJ'-i-kəl).

A *pedagogue* (PED'-ə-gog) is a teacher. But from its original, neutral meaning it has deteriorated to the point where it refers, today, to a narrow-minded, strait-laced, old-fashioned, dogmatic teacher. It is a word of contempt and should be used with caution.

(The *ped*- you see in words like *pedestal, pedal*, and *pedestrian* is from the Latin *pes, pedis*, foot, and despite the identical spelling in English has no relationship to Greek *paidos*.)

Like *pedagogue, demagogue* (DEM'-ə-gog) has also deteriorated in meaning. By derivation a leader (*agogos*) of the people (*demos*), a *demagogue* today is an agitator, a politician who is a rabble-rouser. Many 'leaders' of the past and present in countries around the world have been accused of *demagoguery* (dem'-ə-GOG'-ə-ri). Adjective: *demagogic* (dem'-ə-GOG'-ik).

3. Skin-deep

The *dermatologist* (dər'-mə-TOL'-ə-jist), whose speciality is *dermatology* (dər'-mə-TOL'-ə-ji), is so named from Greek *derma*, skin. Adjective: *dermatological* (dər'-mə-tə-LOJ'-kəl).

See the syllables *derma* in any English word and you will know there is some reference to *skin* – for example, a *hypodermic* (hī-pə-DəR'-mik) needle penetrates *under* (Greek, *hypo*), the *skin*; a *taxidermist* (TAKS'-i-dər-mist), whose business is *taxidermy* (TAKS'-i-dər-mi), prepares, stuffs, and mounts the *skins* of animals; a *pachyderm* (PAK'-i-dərm) is an animal with an unusually thick *skin*, like an elephant, hippopotamus, or rhinoceros; and *dermatitis* (dər-mə-TĪ'-tis) is the general name for any *skin* inflammation, irritation, or infection.

4. The eyes have it

Ophthalmologist (of'-thal-MOL'-ə-jist) – note the *ph* preceding *th* – is from Greek *ophthalmos*, eye, plus *logos*, science or study. The speciality is *ophthalmology* (of'-thal-MOL'-ə-ji), the adjective *ophthalmological* (of'-thal-mə-LOJ'-i-kəl).

An earlier title for this physician is *oculist* (OK'-yoo-list), from Latin *oculus*, eye, a root on which the following English words are also built:

1. *ocular* (OK'-yoo-lə) – an adjective that refers to the eye
2. *monocle* (MON'-ə-kəl) – a lens for one (*monos*) eye, sported as a symbol of the British upper-class male
3. *binoculars* (bi-NOK'-yoo-ləz) – field glasses that increase the range of two (*bi-*) eyes
4. And, strangely enough, *inoculate* (in-OK'-yoo-layt'), a word commonly misspelt with two *n*s. When you are *inoculated* against a disease, an 'eye', puncture, or hole is made in your skin, through which serum is injected.

Do not confuse the *ophthalmologist*, a medical specialist, with two other practitioners who deal with the eye – the *optometrist* (op-TOM'-ə-trist) and *optician* (op-TISH'-ən).

Optometrists are not doctors, and do not perform surgery or administer drugs; they do eye tests and prescribe and fit glasses.

Opticians fall into two categories. The first type, often called *ophthalmic opticians*, perform the same functions as *optometrists*. The second type make or dispense glasses and contact lenses. They fill an *optometrist*'s or *ophthalmologist*'s prescription, grinding and fitting lenses according to specifications; they do not examine patients.

Optometrist combines Greek *opsis*, *optikos*, sight or vision, with *metron*, measurement – the *optometrist*, by etymology, is one who measures vision. The speciality is *optometry* (op-TOM'-ə-tri).

Review of etymology

Write in the space provided an English word that uses each prefix, root, or suffix.

1. *gyne*	woman	_____
2. *paidos*	child	_____
3. *agogos*	leading, leader	_____
4. *derma*	skin	_____
5. *ophthalmos*	eye	_____
6. *oculus*	eye	_____
7. *bi–*	two	_____
8. *-ician*	expert	_____
9. *opsis, optikos*	vision, sight	_____
10. *metron*	measurement	_____

Can you match the words?

1. gynaecology	a. rhinoceros
2. obstetrics	b. stuffing of skins of animals
3. paediatrics	c. speciality dealing with delivering babies
4. pedagogue	d. stirring up discontent among the masses
5. demagoguery	e. one who measures eyesight
6. dermatology	f. speciality dealing with the female reproductive system
7. taxidermy	g. speciality dealing with the treatment of children
8. pachyderm	h. treatment of skin diseases
9. ophthalmologist	i. eye doctor
10. optometrist	j. teacher

Key: 1-f, 2-c, 3-g, 4-j, 5-d, 6-h, 7-b, 8-a, 9-i, 10-e

Do you understand the words?

1. Does a treatise on *obstetrics* deal with childbirth?	YES	NO
2. Does *gynaecology* deal with the diseases of the bloodstream?	YES	NO
3. Is *paediatrics* concerned with premature babies?	YES	NO
4. Does *pedagogy* refer to teaching?	YES	NO

5. Is a *demagogue* a fluent speaker?   YES NO
6. Is a lion a *pachyderm*?   YES NO
7. Is *dermatitis* an inflammation of one of the limbs?   YES NO
8. Is a *taxidermist* a medical practitioner?   YES NO
9. Is an *ophthalmologist* a medical doctor?   YES NO
10. Is an *optometrist* a medical doctor?   YES NO

Key: 1-Y, 2-N, 3-Y, 4-Y, 5-Y, 6-N, 7-N, 8-N, 9-Y, 10-N

SESSION 33 – MORE DOCTORS

1. The straighteners

The *orthopaedist* (aw-thə-PEE'-dist) is so called from the Greek roots
orthos, straight or correct, and *paidos*, child. The *orthopaedist*, by
etymology, straightens children. But today the speciality of *orthopae-
dics* (aw-thə-PEE'-diks) treats deformities, injuries, and diseases of the
bones and joints (of adults as well as children), usually by surgical
procedures. Adjective: *orthopaedic* (aw-thə-PEE'-dik).

Orthodontics (aw-thə-DON'-tiks), the straightening of teeth, is built
on *orthos* plus *odontos*, tooth. The *orthodontist* (aw-thə-DON'-tist)
specializes in improving your 'bite', retracting 'buck teeth', and by
means of braces and other techniques seeing to it that every tooth
is exactly where it belongs in your mouth. Adjective: *orthodontic*
(aw-thə-DON'-tik).

2. The heart

Cardiologist (kah-di-OL'-ə-jist) combines Greek *kardia*, heart, and
logos, science. The speciality is *cardiology* (kah-di-OL'-ə-ji), the adjective *cardiological* (kah'-di-ə-LOJ'-i-kəl).

So a *cardiac* (KAH'-di-ak) condition refers to some malfunctioning
of the heart; a *cardiogram* (KAH'-di-ə-gram') is an electrically produced record of the heartbeat (often called ECG, for ElectroCardio-
Gram). The instrument that produces this record is called a
cardiograph (KAH'-di-ə-grahf').

3. The blood

The *haematologist* (hee-mə-TOL'-ə-jist) is so called from Greek *haima*,
haimatos, blood. Speciality: *haematology* (hee-mə-TOL'-ə-ji); adjective *haematological* (hee'-mə-tə-LOJ'-i-kəl).

The same root is found in *haemophilia* (hee-mə-FIL'-i-ə), with
Greek *philein*, to love; literally, loving blood, but actually a disorder in

which the blood does not clot properly. *Haematoma* (hee-mə-TŌ-mə) is the technical word for a bruise.

4. The nervous system

Neurologist (nyoor-OL'-ə-jist) derives from Greek *neuron*, nerve. Speciality: *neurology* (nyoor(or nyooər)-OL'-ə-ji); adjective: *neurological* (nyoor-ə-LOJ'-i-kəl).

Neuralgia (nyoor-AL'-jə) is acute pain along the nerves and their branches; the word comes from *neuron* plus *algos*, pain.

Neuritis (nyoor-Ī'-tis) is inflammation of the nerves. *Itis* is a suffix meaning *inflammation of*, as in *appendicitis*.

Teaser questions for the amateur etymologist – 8

1. Thinking of the roots *odontos* and *paidos* (spelled *paed-* in English), work out the meaning of *paedodontics*.

2. Recall the roots *kardia* and *algos*. What is the meaning of *cardialgia*?

3. Of *odontalgia*?

4. What is the meaning and derivation of *carditis*?

5. An *analgesic* is a drug given to relieve pain. Can you comment on its derivation?

(*Answers in Chapter 11*)

---

5. The mind

Neurosis (nyoor-O'-sis), combining *neuron* with *-osis*, a suffix meaning *abnormal or diseased condition*, is not, despite its etymology, a disorder of the nerves, but rather a mild mental disorder, with symptoms such as anxiety, depression, or obsessive behaviour. *Neurotic* (nyoor-OT'-ik) is both the adjectival form and the term for a person suffering from *neurosis*.

A full-blown mental disorder is called a *psychosis* (sī-KŌ'-sis), a word built on Greek *psyche*, spirit, soul, or mind, plus *-osis*. A true *psychotic* (sī-KOT'-ik) has lost contact with reality – at least with reality as most of us perceive it, though no doubt *psychotic* (note that this word, like *neurotic*, is both a noun and an adjective) people have their own form of reality.

Built on *psyche* plus *iatreia*, medical healing, a *psychiatrist* (sī-KI'-ə-trist), by etymology, is a mind-healer. The speciality is *psychiatry* (sī-KI'-ə-tri); the adjective is *psychiatric* (sī-ki-AT'-rik).

6. Old people

The doctor who treats old people is a *geriatrician* (jer'-i-ə-TRISH'-ən).
The speciality is *geriatrics* (jer'-i-AT'-riks); the adjective is *geriatric*
(jer'-i-AT'-rik). The Greek root is *geras*, old age.

A related medical speciality is *gerontology* (jer-on-TOL'-ə-ji), which
is the study of the process of ageing and the problems of old age. It
derives from Greek *geron, gerontos*, old man, plus *logos*.

Review of etymology

Write in the space provided an English word that uses each prefix,
root, or suffix.

1. *orthos*	straight, correct	_____
2. *paidos* (*paed-*)	child	_____
3. *odontos*	tooth	_____
4. *kardia*	heart	_____
5. *neuron*	nerve	_____
6. *-osis*	abnormal or diseased condition	_____
7. *-itis*	inflammation	_____
8. *psyche*	spirit, soul, mind	_____
9. *iatreia*	medical healing	_____
10. *geras*	old age	_____

Can you match the words?

1. orthopaedics	a. record of heart beats
2. orthodontics	b. speciality dealing with medical problems of the elderly
3. neuralgia	c. treatment of personality disorders
4. neuritis	d. nerve pain
5. geriatrics	e. treatment of bone problems
6. cardiogram	f. inflammation of the nerves
7. cardiograph	g. mental unbalance
8. neurosis	h. emotional disturbance
9. psychosis	i. straightening of teeth
10. psychiatry	j. instrument for recording heartbeats

Key: 1-e, 2-i, 3-d, 4-f, 5-b, 6-a, 7-j, 8-h, 9-g, 10-c

Do you understand the words?

1.	A *gynaecologist*'s patients are mostly men	YES NO
2.	*Ophthalmology* is the study of eye diseases	YES NO
3.	*Orthopaedics* is the speciality dealing with the bones and joints	YES NO
4.	A *cardiac* patient has a heart ailment	YES NO
5.	A person with a bad 'bite' may profit from *orthodontics*	YES NO
6.	*Neuralgia* is a disease of the bones	YES NO
7.	A *neurosis* is the same as a *psychosis*	YES NO
8.	*Neuritis* is inflammation of the nerves	YES NO
9.	*Psychiatric* treatment is designed to relieve tension, fears, and insecurities	YES NO
10.	A *geriatrician* has very young patients	YES NO

Key: 1-N, 2-Y, 3-Y, 4-Y, 5-Y, 6-N, 7-N, 8-Y, 9-Y, 10-N

Becoming word-conscious

Perhaps, if you have been working as assiduously with this book as I hope you have, you have noticed an interesting phenomenon.

This phenomenon is as follows: you read a magazine article and suddenly you see one or more of the words you have recently learned. Or you open a book and there again are some of the words you have been working with. In short, all your reading seems to call to your attention the very words you've been studying.

CHAPTER 9
THE WORLD OF WORK – EXPERTS
AND PROFESSIONALS

Most people spend part of every working day at some gainful employment, honest or otherwise, and in so doing often contribute their little mite to the progress of the world. We explore in this chapter the ideas behind people's occupations.

1. Behaviour

By education and training, this practitioner is an expert in human behaviour – what makes people act as they do, how they perceive the world, why they have certain feelings, how their personalities were formed – in short, what makes them tick.

> A *psychologist*

2. Bones and blood vessels

This practitioner is a member of the profession that originated in 1874, when Andrew T. Still devised a drugless technique of curing diseases by massage and other manipulative procedures, a technique based on the theory that illness may be caused by the undue pressure of displaced bones on nerves and blood vessels.

> An *osteopath*

3. Feet

This practitioner treats minor foot ailments – corns, calluses, bunions, fallen arches, etc.

> A *chiropodist*

4. Just what the doctor ordered

This professional is trained in the chemical composition of medicinal drugs; he or she makes up each compound and dispenses it to the patient. He or she may also give advice on straightforward medical problems.

A *pharmacist*

5.   Getting back into shape

This practitioner supplements the orthopaedic surgeon's work, by getting the patient fit again through a programme of carefully designed exercises.

A *physiotherapist*

6.   A view of the interior

This practitioner operates the X-ray machine that gives the physician or surgeon a picture of whatever is relevant in the inside of the patient.

A *radiographer*

7.   A calculated risk

This professional is employed by an insurance company, bank, or building society to calculate risks, and to work out appropriate premiums, dividends, annuities, etc.

An *actuary*

8.   Understanding money

This professional may be an academic, or may work for a bank or other financial institution. He or she is an expert in the science of the way a country's financial life works; inflation, unemployment, interest rates, balance of payments – these are the factors in this professional daily round.

An *economist*

9.   Looking things over

This professional inspects buildings to determine their condition or value, or maps terrain before building work starts.

A *surveyor*

10.   Bricks and mortar

This professional designs buildings of any sort or size, whether made of stone, bricks, concrete, glass or whatever, or any combination of these. The inside layout and fittings of the building are also the concern of this professional.

An *architect*

Can you match the words?

1. chiropodist	a. designer of buildings and interiors
2. architect	b. risk calculator
3. actuary	c. manipulator of bones
4. radiographer	d. drug dispenser
5. psychologist	e. exercise healer
6. pharmacist	f. assessor of buildings
7. surveyor	g. financial expert
8. osteopath	h. X-ray expert
9. physiotherapist	i. one who studies human behaviour
10. economist	j. foot healer

Key: 1-j, 2-a, 3-b, 4-h, 5-i, 6-d, 7-f, 8-c, 9-e, 10-g

Do you understand the words?

1. A *psychologist* treats corns and bunions   YES NO
2. An *osteopath* prescribes and fits glasses   YES NO
3. An *economist* predicts trends in inflation   YES NO
4. You go to a *pharmacist* to have your prescription made up   YES NO
5. A *chiropodist* specializes in straightening teeth   YES NO
6. A *radiographer* has a good knowledge of the skeleton YES NO
7. You would go to an *actuary* for active exercises to get you fit   YES NO
8. An *architect* must be good at drawing   YES NO
9. A *physiotherapist* is an expert in child behaviour   YES NO
10. A *surveyor* is a kind of grocer   YES NO

Key: 1-N, 2-N, 3-Y, 4-Y, 5-N, 6-Y, 7-N, 8-Y, 9-N, 10-N

SESSION 35 – ALL IN THE MIND

Psychologist (sī-KOL'-ə-jist) is built upon the same Greek root as *psychiatrist* – *psyche*, spirit, soul, or mind. In *psychiatrist*, the combining form is *iatreia*, medical healing. In *psychologist*, the combining form is *logos*, science or study; a *psychologist*, by etymology, is one who studies the mind. A psychologist has a scientific rather than a medical training, and will specialize, e.g. in *educational psychology* (the study of why children do or don't get on well at school), or *industrial psychology* (the study of the mental effects of the work-place).

The field is *psychology* (sī-KOL'-ə-ji), the adjective *psychological* (sī-kə-LOJ'-i-kəl).

Psyche (SĪ-ki) is also an English word in its own right – it designates the mental life, the spiritual or non-physical aspect of one's existence. The adjective *psychic* (SĪ'-kik) refers to phenomena or qualities that cannot be explained in purely physical terms. People may be called *psychic* if they seem to possess a sixth sense, a special gift of mind reading, or any mysterious aptitudes that cannot be accounted for logically. A person's disturbance is *psychic* if it is emotional or mental, rather than physical.

Psyche combines with the Greek *pathos*, suffering or disease, to form *psychopathic* (sī-kə-PATH'-ik), an adjective that describes someone suffering from a severe mental or emotional disorder. A *psychopath* (SĪ'-kə-path'), sometimes called a *psychopathic personality*, appears to be lacking an inner moral censor, and often commits criminal acts, without anxiety or guilt, in order to obtain immediate gratification of desires.

The root *psyche* combines with Greek *soma*, body, to form *psychosomatic* (sī'-kō-sə-MAT'-ik), an adjective that delineates the powerful influence that the mind, especially the unconscious, has on the state of the body. A *psychosomatic* disorder actually exists insofar as symptoms are concerned (headache, excessive urination, pains, paralysis, heart palpitations), yet there is no organic cause within the body. The cause is within the *psyche*, the mind. A related word is *psychogenic* (sī-kō-JEN'-ik), of psychic origin, from the Greek root *genesis*, origin.

Psychoanalysis (sī-kō-ə-NAL'-ə-sis) relies on the technique of deeply, exhaustively probing into the unconscious, a technique developed by Sigmund Freud. In oversimplified terms, the general principle of *psychoanalysis* is to guide the patient to an awareness of the deep-seated, unconscious causes of anxieties, fears, conflicts, and tension. Once the causes are found and thoroughly understood, claim the *psychoanalysts*, the anxieties, etc. may (but not necessarily) subsequently disappear.

There are many different schools of psychoanalysis apart from the classic Freudian version. Among them are the *Jungian* (after Carl Jung, who introduced the terms *introvert* and *extrovert*, see Session 23), the *Kleinian* (after Melanie Klein, specialist in child patients), and the *Reichian* (after Wilhelm Reich, who emphasized sex).

A less precise discipline is *psychotherapy* (sī-kō-THER'-ə-pi), which means more or less any means of treating psychological disorders through a verbal approach. The Greek word *therapeia*, as noted earlier, means care or attendance of a non-medical sort. A *psychotherapist* (sī-kō-THER'-ə-pist) is not a doctor; nor are the practitioners of *aromatherapy*, treatment with fragrant oils (from Latin *aroma*, fragrance), or *homeopathy*, treatment with very small quantities of the substance that causes the same symptoms that the patient shows (from Greek *homoio-*, the same, plus *pathos*, disease).

Review of etymology

Write in the space provided an English word that uses each prefix, root, or suffix.

1.	*psyche*	spirit, soul, mind	_____
2.	*iatreia*	medical healing	_____
3.	*-ic*	adjective suffix	_____
4.	*soma*	body	_____
5.	*genesis*	birth, origin	_____
6.	*pathos*	suffering, disease	_____
7.	*therapeia*	care, attendance	_____
8.	*intro-*	inwards	_____
9.	*-ist*	noun suffix	_____
10.	*homeo-*	the same	_____

Can you match the words?

1.	psychology	a.	mental or emotional disturbance
2.	psyche	b.	psychological treatment based on Freudian techniques
3.	psychic	c.	general term for non-technical psychological treatment
4.	psychopathy	d.	originating in the mind or emotions
5.	psychosomatic	e.	medical treatment of mental symptoms, e.g. with drugs
6.	psychoanalysis	f.	one's inner or mental life, or self-image
7.	psychogenic	g.	study of the human mind and behaviour
8.	psychotherapy	h.	describing the interaction of mind and body
9.	psychopath	i.	pertaining to the mind; extrasensory
10.	psychiatry	j.	person lacking in social conscience or inner censor

Key: 1-g, 2-f, 3-i, 4-a, 5-h, 6-b, 7-d, 8-c, 9-j, 10-e

Do you understand the words?

1. *Psychological* treatment aims at sharpening the intellect   YES NO
2. *Psychic* phenomena can be explained on rational or physical grounds   YES NO
3. *Psychopathic* personalities are normal and healthy   YES NO
4. A *psychosomatic* symptom is caused by organic disease   YES NO
5. Every therapist uses *psychoanalysis*   YES NO
6. A *psychogenic* illness originates in the mind or emotions   YES NO
7. A *psychotherapist* must have a medical degree   YES NO
8. *Psychoanalytically* oriented therapy uses Freudian techniques   YES NO
9. A *psychopath* is often a criminal   YES NO
10. *Homeopathy* is a branch of medicine   YES NO

Key: 1-N, 2-N, 3-N, 4-N, 5-N, 6-Y, 7-N, 8-Y, 9-Y, 10-N

SESSION 36 – PARAMEDICALS

1. Bones, feet, and hands

Osteopath (OS'-ti-ǝ-path) combines Greek *osteon*, bone, with *pathos*, suffering, disease. *Osteopathy* (os'-ti-OP'-ǝ-thi) was originally based on the theory that disease is caused by pressure of the bones on blood vessels and nerves. An *osteopathic* (os'-ti-ǝ-PATH'-ik) practitioner is *not* a bone specialist, despite the misleading etymology (and despite the fact that many people with bad backs are treated by osteopaths) – and should not be confused with the *orthopaedist*, who is.

The *chiropodist* (ki-ROP'-ǝ-dist) (Greek *cheir*, hand, spelt *chiro-* in English, plus *pous*, *podos*, foot) practises chiropody (ki-ROP'-ǝ-di). The term was coined in the days before labour-saving machinery and push-button devices, when people worked manually and developed calluses on their hands as well as on their feet.

The root *pous*, *podos* is also found in:

1. *octopus* (OK'-tǝ-pǝs), the eight-armed (or, as the etymology has it, eight-footed) sea creature (Greek *okto*, eight).

2. *platypus* (PLAT'-i-pǝs), the strange water mammal with a duck's bill, webbed feet, and a beaver-like tail that reproduces by laying eggs (Greek *platy*, broad, flat – hence, by etymology, a flatfoot).

3. *podium* (PŌ'-di-əm), a speaker's platform, etymologically a place for the feet. (The suffix *-ium* often signifies 'place where', as in *gymnasium, stadium, auditorium,* etc.)

4. *tripod* (TRĪ'-pod), a three-legged (or 'footed') stand for a camera or other device (*tri-*, three).

5. *podiatrist* (pō-DĪ'-ə-trist), another name for a *chiropodist*. The speciality is *podiatry* (pō-DĪ'-ə-tri).

2. A medical chemist

A *pharmacist* (FAR'-mə-sist) is by training a scientist who knows about the chemical composition of drugs, and how to make them. The derivation is from Greek *pharmakon*, a drug or potion. The place where drugs are dispensed is a *pharmacy* (FAR'-mə-si). An old word for a pharmacist is an *apothecary* (ə-POTH'-ə-kə-ri), which is from the Greek for a store-cupboard (*apotheke*).

The scientist who studies the way drugs act within the body is a *pharmacologist* (far-mə-KOL'-ə-jist), of which you can work out the derivation. The enormous multi-national industry that develops and manufactures drugs is called the *pharmaceutical* industry, from Greek *pharmakeus*, a person who sells drugs (or, a poisoner!).

3. *Mens sana in corpore sano*

The Latin tag above means 'a healthy mind in a healthy body'. But the derivation of *physiotherapist* (fi'-zi-ō-THER'-ə-pist) is from Greek: *physis*, the natural form of something, hence the body, plus *therapeia*. Physiotherapy is just one of a range of treatments carried out by skilled practitioners other than doctors. *Hydrotherapy* (hī-drō-THER'-ə-pi) is treatment with water, in which patients with weak joints or muscles do exercises in water, i.e. in a special pool (from Greek *hydr-*, water). *Chemotherapy* (KEE'-mō-ther'-ə-pi) – treatment with chemicals – and *radiotherapy* (RAY'-di-ō-ther'-ə-pi) – treatment with radiation – are both used for patients recovering from cancer.

4. Radiation and writing

Radio- in combination does not mean radio as in a radio broadcast, but *radiation* of any sort (sunlight, X-rays, etc.); the root is Latin *radius*, a ray (or a spoke in a wheel; think back to school geometry).

The *radiographer* (ray'-di-OG'-rə-fə) is the person who utilizes X-rays (a form of radiation) to obtain pictures of the body's interior. The derivation is a Latin–Greek combination (disliked by purists) of Latin *radius* with Greek *graphein*, to write; thus *radiography* is literally 'written with radiation'.

The root *graphein* comes up time and again in English words, in both technical and everyday language:

1. *cardiograph* (discussed in Session 33) – etymologically, a 'heart writer' (*kardia*, heart)

2. *photograph* – 'written by light' (Greek *photos*, light)

3. *phonograph* – a 'sound writer' (Greek *phone*, sound); this word was the forerunner of *gramophone*, itself now obsolete

4. *telegraph* – a 'distance writer' (Greek *tele-*, far, at a distance)

5. *biography* – 'life writing' (Greek *bios*, life); hence *autobiography*, 'self life writing' (Greek *auto-*, oneself)

6. *calligraphy* – 'beautiful writing' (Greek *kallos*, beauty)

7. *choreography* – 'dance writing' (Greek *khoros*, dancing); this is the art of arranging the steps and formations of the dancers in a ballet. Note that the same Greek root *khoros* has also given us *chorus*, a group of people singing; in an ancient Greek play the *chorus* would both dance and sing as they commented on the actions of the main characters.

Review of etymology

Write in the space provided an English word that uses each prefix, root, or suffix.

1. *osteon*	bone	_____
2. *pathos*	suffering, disease	_____
3. *pous, podos*	foot	_____
4. *okto*	eight	_____
5. *-ium*	place where	_____
6. *tri-*	three	_____
7. *cheir* (*chiro-*)	hand	_____
8. *-graphy*	writing	_____
9. *pharm-*	drug	_____
10. *radio-*	radiation	_____

Can you match the words?

1. podium	a. drugs workshop
2. osteopathy	b. ballet design
3. pharmacy	c. chart of heart function
4. chiropody	d. egg-laying water mammal
5. platypus	e. treatment of feet
6. pharmacology	f. exercises in water

7. cardiograph   g. speaker's platform
8. choreography   h. person who makes up drugs
9. hydrotherapy   i. the science of drug action
10. apothecary   j. treatment by manipulation of bones

Key: 1-g, 2-j, 3-a, 4-e, 5-d, 6-i, 7-c, 8-b, 9-f, 10-h

Do you understand the words?

1. *Chiropody* and *podiatry* are synonymous	YES	NO
2. A *calligrapher* makes a work of art out of written material	YES	NO
3. A *tripod* has four legs	YES	NO
4. A *radiographer* works in a hospital	YES	NO
5. You take your prescription to the *podium*	YES	NO
6. *Hydrotherapy* is a treatment for cancer	YES	NO
7. A *pharmacist* uses X-rays	YES	NO
8. A famous person is likely to write an *autobiography*	YES	NO
9. *Physiotherapy* involves physical exercises to bring the patient back to health	YES	NO
10. The *pharmaceutical* industry is concerned with farming	YES	NO

Key: 1-Y, 2-Y, 3-N, 4-Y, 5-N, 6-N, 7-N, 8-Y, 9-Y, 10-N

SESSION 37 – MONEY AND REAL ESTATE

1. How to calculate the risks

We saw (Session 34) that a professional who works out risks and premiums for an insurance company, etc. is called an *actuary* (AK'-tyoo-ə-ri). This word comes to us straight from the Latin *actuarius*, a person who deals with *acta*, public business (or acts). The adjective is *actuarial*.

Most of the English words that begin with *act-* are from this same family of Latin roots: *ago*, to do, with its past tense *actus*, something that is done. Thus we have words such as *active*, *action*, *activity*, all embodying this idea.

You will not confuse the actuary with the *actor* or the *activist* (someone whose political beliefs lead them to take militant *action*).

2. Money makes the world go round

The *economist* (ee-KON'-ə-mist) is the expert on the interlocking machinery of a country's financial systems. The word is built on two useful Greek roots. The first is *oikos*, home (words derived from this used to be written *oeco-* in English; you might perhaps come across a very old book in which economist was spelt *oeconomist*). The science (or perhaps it should be called an art) practised by economists is *economics* (ee-kə-NOM'-iks).

We find the same root in *ecology* (ee-KOL'-ə-ji), which literally means 'home science' but actually means the study of how living things fit together in their 'home', i.e. their natural environment.

Teaser questions for the amateur etymologist – 9

1. Latin *octoginta* is related to Greek *okto*, eight (as in octopus). How old is an *octogenarian* (ok'-tə-ji-NAIR'-i-ən)?

2. When practising a difficult part, a musician is ruled by a device called a *metronome* (MET'-rə-nōm). What is its derivation, and its literal meaning?

3. If the suffix *-mancy* comes from a Greek word meaning *foretelling* or *prediction*, can you work out what *chiromancy* (KĪ'-rə-man'-si) must be?

4. You remember that the derivation of *sympathize* is from Greek *sym-*, with, and *pathos*, feeling. Can you guess what the word is for 'feeling at a distance'?

5. Can you guess what the science of *psychometrics* (sī'-kō-MET'-riks) is concerned with, and what its methods are?

(Answers in Chapter 11)

The other root in *economist* is Greek *nomos*, rule or law. Thus economics is the study of the rules that make our country 'tick'. A number of areas of knowledge have names ending in *-nomy*, as for instance *agronomy*, from Latin *ager* (a field), knowledge of the rules of farming (as distinct from *agriculture* which is actually doing it).

Within the science of economics, a person might specialize in *econometrics* (ee'-kon-ə-MET'-riks), which is the study of key economic measurements, as for example the rate of inflation or the public sector borrowing requirement, and how these relate to each other mathematically. Here we have a third Greek root, *metron*, a measurement.

This is a very useful root, occurring in many English words, often as the suffix -*meter*, something that measures:

1. *thermometer* (ther-MOM'-i-tə) – 'heat measurer' (Greek *therme*, heat).

2. *barometer* (bə-ROM'-i-tə) – literally, 'weight measurer' (Greek *baros*, weight), but actually a device to measure atmospheric pressure.

3. *chronometer* (krə-NOM'-i-tə) – 'time measurer', used of something more accurate and technical than a mere wristwatch (Greek *chronos*, time; see other related words in Session 12).

4. *anenometer* (an-ə-MOM'-i-tə) – 'wind measurer' (Greek *anemos*, wind).

3.   Bricks and mortar

The person who prepares plans of building sites is called a *surveyor* (ser-VAY'-ə). This word is from Latin origins: the prefix *sur-* is derived from Latin *super*, meaning over, and the -*vey*- is from *video*, to see. So a surveyor is a person who looks over the site. The same elements are also found in *supervisor*, a person who 'oversees' or is in charge of something.

Usually English words that are based on *video*, to see, have it in its past form, -*vise* or -*vision* (i.e. something seen). Thus we have *revise*, to look at something again (prefix *re-*, again), *visionary*, a person with foresight or far-reaching ideals, or *television*, something that sees at a distance (a Greek–Latin combination; Greek *tele-*, far).

But the -*vey*- form of *video* does crop up elsewhere. We have it in *purveyor*, a person who supplies food and provisions. In derivation this word is identical to one who *provides*, i.e. one who foresees the need for something (Latin prefix *pro-*, before, plus *videre*). It is a good word to use figuratively: 'A notorious purveyor of misinformation.'

As you know, the professional who designs buildings is an *architect* (ARK'-i-tekt). This time the derivation is Greek. The root *arch-* means chief, or ruler (and we have met it before, in words such as matriarch – see Session 15); it is familiar in such formations as *archbishop*, the chief bishop, or *archangel*. The other root is Greek *tekton*, a workman, which in turn is derived from the immensely important Greek word *tekhne*, meaning skill, art, craftsmanship, etc. From it we get all our words such as *technology* (literally, the science of skills), *technician* (a skilled person), and *technophobia* (fear of technical things – see Appendix).

And to end this Session with a bang – *pyrotechnics* – fireworks! (From Greek *pyr*, fire.)

Review of etymology

Write in the space provided an English word that uses each prefix, root, or suffix.

1. *super-*   over, above   _____
2. *-nomy*   study of laws of   _____
3. *-meter*   something that measures _____
4. *-vise*   to see   _____
5. *sur-*   above   _____
6. *eco-*   home, environment   _____
7. *techn-*   skill, craftsmanship   _____
8. *arch-, -arch* chief, ruler   _____
9. *agr-*   field, farming   _____
10. *pyro-*   fire   _____

Can you match the words?

1. purveyor   a. fireworks
2. barometer   b. accurate timepiece
3. pyrotechnics   c. person who calculates risks
4. visionary   d. political agitator
5. econometrics   e. an idealist
6. ecology   f. someone who sells provisions
7. supervisor   g. pressure gauge
8. actuary   h. foreman
9. chronometer   i. study of financial statistics
10. activist   j. study of plants and animals
                        in their environment

Key: 1-f, 2-g, 3-a, 4-e, 5-i, 6-j, 7-h, 8-c, 9-b, 10-d

Do you understand the words?

1. *Ecology* is the study of farming   YES NO
2. An *actuary* is interested in politics   YES NO
3. You use a *barometer* to forecast a change in the
   weather   YES NO
4. To study *econometrics* you need to be good at
   mathematics   YES NO
5. A *purveyor* is a kind of legal executive   YES NO
6. A *visionary* is a person in charge at the works   YES NO

7. A matriarch is a female *architect*   YES NO
8. *Economics* is the science of finance   YES NO
9. When you *revise*, you take a second look at what
   you have studied   YES NO
10. *Technophobia* is fear of spiders   YES NO

Key: 1-N, 2-N, 3-Y, 4-Y, 5-N, 6-N, 7-N, 8-Y, 9-Y, 10-N

Getting used to new words

I have already alerted you to the intimate relationship between reading and vocabulary building. Good books and the better magazines will not only acquaint you with a host of new ideas (and, therefore, new words, since every word is the verbalization of an idea), but also will help you gain a more complete and a richer understanding of the hundreds of words you are learning through your work in this book. If you have been doing a sufficient amount of stimulating reading – and that means, at minimum, several magazines a week and at least three books of non-fiction a month – you have been meeting, constantly, over and over again, the new words you have been learning in these pages. Every such encounter is like seeing an old friend in a new place.

CHAPTER 10
EXPLORERS OF KNOWLEDGE – SCIENCE AND SCIENTISTS

A true scientist lives up to the etymological meaning of the title 'one who knows'. Anything scientific is based on facts – observable facts that can be recorded, tested, checked, and verified.

Science, then, deals with human knowledge – as far as it has gone. It has gone very far indeed since its beginnings in ancient times, when the great Greek scientist Aristotle sought to write down all that was known about the natural world.

Who are some of the more important explorers of knowledge – and by what terms are they known?

SESSION 38 – TEN FIELDS OF ENQUIRY

1. The queen of the sciences

Some say that this is not a science at all, some call it the queen of the sciences. It is the study of number, shape and space, their meaning and interrelationships.

Mathematics

2. The nature of all things

The field is the basic nature of the material world – what it is made of, and how each part interacts with every other, on all levels from the invisibly small to the invisibly large.

Physics

3. What's above?

The field is the heavens and all that's in them – planets, galaxies, stars, and other universes.

Astronomy

4. And what's below?

The field is the comparatively little and insignificant whirling ball on which we live – the Earth. How did our planet come into being, what is it made of, how were its mountains, oceans, rivers, plains, and valleys formed, and what lies deep beneath the Earth's crust?

Geology

5. Whatever the weather

The field is the earth's atmosphere, and how we can understand the processes that give rise to changes in the weather. This science looks at both normal weather patterns and the exceptional catastrophic events.

Meteorology

6. What is life?

The field is all living organisms – from the simplest one-celled amoeba to the amazingly complex and mystifying structure we call a human being. Plant or animal, flesh or vegetable, denizen of water, earth, or air – if it lives and grows, this is where it is studied.

Biology

7. Flora

Biology classifies life into two great divisions – plant and animal. This science's province is the former category – flowers, trees, shrubs, mosses, marine vegetation, blossoms, fruits, seeds, grasses, and all the rest that make up the plant kingdom.

Botany

8. And Fauna

Animals of every description, kind and condition, from birds to bees, fish to fowl, reptiles to humans, are the special area of exploration of this science.

Zoology

9. And all the little bugs

There are over a million different species of insects so far described, and scientists estimate that there may be three times as many still to be discovered. This science is dedicated to finding out more about all insects, known and unknown.

Entomology

10. Times past

The field is the past record of mankind – from the time we first evolved from our ape-like ancestors to the recent past when we became industrialists. Much of the evidence used in this science is dug up from under the ground, but there are other techniques too, such as aerial photography.

Archaeology

What is the scientist called?

You will have noticed that most of the sciences have a name that ends in *-logy*; this, as already noted, is from the Greek *logos*, meaning word or knowledge. Persons who study a science ending in *-logy* are called *-logists*; some examples are given below.

But there is another large group of sciences whose names end in *-graphy*; this comes from the Greek *graphein*, to write, so that these sciences are literally 'the writing of . . .', or more accurately, 'the description of . . .'. One example is *geography*, the description of the Earth. The practitioner always ends *-grapher*, e.g. *geographer*.

Less common are sciences ending *-nomy*. We saw in the last Session that this is from the Greek word *nomos*, rule, law. Here we have *astronomy*, to add to *agronomy* that we met earlier. Unfortunately, the way to form the name for the scientist is irregular, being sometimes *-nomer* and sometimes *-nomist*. See table below.

Finally there are many sciences whose names end in *-ics*. This is just an all-purpose noun ending, coming from Greek via Latin. In the list above we have *mathematics* and *physics*. Once again the name of the scientist is irregular: sometimes it goes *-ician*, sometimes *-icist*.

Science	*Scientist*
meteorology	meteorologist (mee'-tyoo-ROL'-ə-jist)
psychology	psychologist (sī-KOL'-ə-jist)
biology	biologist (bī-OL'-ə-jist)
geography	geographer (jee-OG'-rə-fə)
oceanography	oceanographer (ō'-shə-NOG'-rə-fə)
agronomy	agronomist (ə-GRON'-ə-mist)
astronomy	astronomer (ə-STRON'-ə-mə)
mathematics	mathematician (math'-ə-mə-TISH'-ən)
physics	physicist (FIZ'-i-sist)

| statistics | statistician (stat-is-TISH'-ən) |
| genetics | geneticist (jə-NET'-i-sist) |

Can you match the words?

1. physics
2. archaeology
3. astronomy
4. mathematics
5. botany
6. entomology

7. geology

8. biology
9. meteorology
10. zoology

a. The science of the plant kingdom
b. The science of humanity's past
c. The science of stars and planets
d. The science of all living creatures
e. The science of insects
f. The science of the basis of the material world
g. The science of the atmosphere and weather
h. The science of number, shape, space
i. The science of the animal kingdom
j. The science of the Earth

Key: 1-f, 2-b, 3-c, 4-h, 5-a, 6-e, 7-j, 8-d, 9-g, 10-i

Do you understand the words?

1. A *physicist* is interested in ants and wasps	YES	NO
2. An *astronomer* works with a telescope	YES	NO
3. A *botanist* would be useful in a pharmaceutical company	YES	NO
4. A *meteorologist* uses a barometer	YES	NO
5. *Mathematics* involves digging things up	YES	NO
6. *Biologists* are only interested in abstract data	YES	NO
7. *Geology* involves data from all over the world	YES	NO
8. You might find an *archaeologist* in an aeroplane	YES	NO
9. *Entomologists* like turning over stones	YES	NO
10. *Zoologists* study crops and vegetables	YES	NO

Key: 1-N, 2-Y, 3-Y, 4-Y, 5-N, 6-N, 7-Y, 8-Y, 9-Y, 10-N

SESSION 39 – THE 'HARD' SCIENCES

1. The Great Learning

Mathematics is not only the queen of the sciences, it also has pole position as far as its name goes. The derivation is from Greek *mathematika*, which simply means *things learnt*, hence *knowledge*. It also appears in English in the word *polymath*, a person who is competent in many fields of learning (the prefix is Greek *poly-*, many).

Modern mathematics contains many special fields, but the three that were traditionally taught at school level all have interesting derivations. *Arithmetic* (ə-RITH'-mə-tik), the manipulation of numerical values, comes straight from the Greek *arithmos*, a number; the person who studies this is an *arithmetician* (a'-rith-mə-TISH'-ən). *Algebra*, doing arithmetic but with abstract symbols (usually letters) instead of actual numbers, is from an Arabic word, *al-jabr*, which originally meant setting broken bones but came to mean any system of putting jumbled-up things in order. The expert in this is an *algebraist* (al-jə-BRAY'-ist). *Geometry*, the study of angles, curves, shapes, etc. is literally 'measurement of the Earth', its roots being Greek *ge*, the Earth (of which more shortly), plus Greek *metron*, measurement. Geometry is now solely a branch of mathematics, and its practitioner is a *geometrician* (jee-om'-ə-TRISH'-ən). Those of you who got on well at school will have come across the *calculus*, an advanced type of algebra dealing with infinitely varying quantities; the word is the same as the Latin for a little pebble, as used for counting in ancient times, and is also the basis for our words *calculate, calculation*, etc.

2. The nature of all things

The Greek word *physis* means the natural form that a thing has, its true nature; from this root we get *physics*, the science of the nature of matter and energy. Branches of physics include:

atomic physics – study of the nature of the *atom*, the basic unit of matter that was at one time thought to be the smallest possible entity – hence its name which literally means 'that which cannot be divided' (from Greek *a-*, not, and *tomaios*, cut off)

nuclear physics – study of the nucleus of the atom. It turned out that the atom was not indivisible after all, but consisted of a dense *nucleus* with a shell of electrons revolving around it (Latin *nucleus*, kernel, from *nux*, nut)

particle physics – study of the particles that make up the nucleus (physicists have given these particles weird names such as *quark, lepton, gluon*)

solid-state physics – study of the nature of matter as it exists in solids in a crystalline form; this has applications in electronics, where circuits are made of crystals of silicon

astrophysics – study of the physical nature of the stars and planets (for derivation, see below)

3. The universe

The study of the entire universe, or indeed of the infinite number of other universes that may exist besides our own, is known as *cosmology* (koz-MOL'-ə-ji), from Greek *kosmos*, universe. The same root is in the adjective *cosmic*, meaning belonging to the whole universe, used literally in *cosmic radiation* or figuratively in *of cosmic importance*.

Astronomy (ə-STRON'-ə-mi) is built on Greek *astron*, star, and *nomos*, law, or order. The *astronomer* (ə-STRON'-ə-mə) is interested in the laws that control the stars and other celestial bodies. The adjective is *astronomical* (as'-trə-NOM'-i-kəl), a word often used in a non-heavenly sense, as in 'the *astronomical* size of the national debt'. *Astronomy* deals in such enormous distances that the adjective *astronomical* is applied to any tremendously large figure.

Astron, star, combines with *logos* to form *astrology* (ə-STROL'-ə-ji), which assesses the influence of planets and stars on human events. The practitioner is an *astrologer* (ə-STROL'-ə-jə); note that this is an exception to the rule that science -*logy* has as its practitioner -*logist* (maybe this reflects astrology's doubtful claim to be a science).

By etymology, an *astronaut* (AS'-trə-nawt') is a 'sailor among the stars' (Greek *nautes*, sailor). This person is termed a *cosmonaut* (KOZ'-mə-nawt') by the Russians, 'sailor in the universe'. *Nautical* (NAWT'-i-kəl), relating to sailors, sailing, ships, or navigation, de-rives also from *nautes*.

Aster (AS'-tə) is a star-shaped flower. *Asterisk* (AS'-tə-risk), a star-shaped symbol (*), is generally used to direct the reader to look for a footnote. *Astrophysics* (as'-trō-FIZ'-iks) is that branch of physics dealing with heavenly bodies.

Disaster (di-ZAHS'-tə) and *disastrous* (di-ZAHS'-trəs) also come from *astron*, star. In ancient times it was believed that the stars ruled human destiny; any misfortune or calamity, therefore, happened to someone because the stars were in opposition. (*Dis-*, a prefix of many meanings, in this word signifies *against*.)

4. The Earth and its life

Geology (jee-OL'-ə-ji) is the science of the Earth; the scientist is a *geologist* (jee-OL'-ə-jist), and the adjective is *geological* (jee-ō-LOJ'-ik-əl). The study focuses on the history of our planet, and the matter that it is composed of.

Geography (jee-(or ji')-OG'-rə-fi) is writing about (*graphein*, to write), or mapping the earth. A practitioner of the science is a *geographer* (jee-(or ji')-OG'-rə-fə), the adjective is *geographic* (jee'-(or ji')-ə-GRAF'-ik). A specialized branch of this is *cartography* (kar-TOG'-rə-fi), making maps (from Latin *charta*, chart or map; ultimately from Greek *kharte*, papyrus, i.e. something to write on).

Modern branches of geology include:

seismology, the study of earthquakes (Greek *seismos*, a shaking, an earthquake; the same root is in Poseidon, god of the sea, whom the Greeks believed to be responsible for earthquakes)

volcanology or *vulcanology*, the study of volcanoes (derived from the name of Vulcan, the Roman god of fire and metalworking; his name occurs again in *vulcanized* rubber, which is hardened by a heat process)

petrology, the study of the nature of rocks (Latin *petra*, a rock; from this root we also get *petroleum*, more usually known as petrol, which is literally 'oil from the rocks' – Latin *petra*, plus *oleum*, oil)

oceanography, the study of the seas and oceans (from the name of the Greek god Oceanos, who was not god of the sea but of a stream of water that was believed to encircle the Earth).

5. The weather

The study of the weather is called *meteorology* (mee'-tyoo-ROL'-ə-ji); what has this to do with *meteors*, otherwise known as shooting stars? These words are derived from Greek *meteoron*, something which is up in the sky. *Meteorologists* (mee'-tyoo-ROL'-ə-jists) now make extensive use of pictures relayed back to Earth from *satellites* (Latin *satelles*, an attendant), but also use traditional ways to measure atmospheric pressure (with a *barometer*), temperature (with a *thermometer*), and wind (with an *anemometer*).

A major branch of meteorology is *hydrology* (hī-DROL'-ə-ji), the study of water in the atmosphere and on Earth (Greek *hydor, hydros*, water). *Hydrologists* study the way that water is evaporated from the oceans and then deposited again as rain or snow, and they also study the causes of floods and droughts.

Review of etymology

Write in the space provided an English word that uses each prefix, root, or suffix.

1. *logos*	science, study	_____
2. *astron*	star	_____
3. *nautes*	sailor	_____
4. *dis-*	against	_____

5. *nomos*	rule, law	_____
6. *hydr-*	water	_____
7. *ge (geo-)*	earth	_____
8. *graphein*	to write	_____
9. *-meter*	measuring device	_____
10. *petra*	rock	_____

Can you match the words?

1. astronaut	a. studies volcanoes
2. cartographer	b. foretells happenings by the stars
3. seismologist	c. 'sailor of the universe'
4. arithmetician	d. manipulates numbers
5. astrophysicist	e. studies the universe
6. vulcanologist	f. foretells the weather
7. cosmologist	g. studies earthquakes
8. meteorologist	h. studies the nature of the stars
9. cosmonaut	i. draws maps
10. astrologer	j. 'sailor of the stars'

Key: 1-j, 2-i, 3-g, 4-d, 5-h, 6-a, 7-e, 8-f, 9-c, 10-b

Do you understand the words?

1. An *aster* might be interesting to a botanist	YES NO
2. Do *petrological* investigations sometimes lead to the discovery of oil?	YES NO
3. A *polymath* is an expert in population figures	YES NO
4. An *astrophysicist* would be interested in samples of dust from Mars	YES NO
5. A *geometrician* is a person who makes maps	YES NO
6. *Meteorology* is the study of meteors	YES NO
7. Are *nautical* manoeuvres carried out at sea?	YES NO
8. An *astrologer* uses a radio-telescope	YES NO
9. A *cosmonaut* travels in a space capsule	YES NO
10. *Algebra* is the science of foretelling disasters	YES NO

Key: 1-Y, 2-Y, 3-N, 4-Y, 5-N, 6-N, 7-Y, 8-N, 9-Y, 10-N

SESSION 40 – THE LIFE SCIENCES

1. What is life?

The science of life in general is *biology* (bī-OL'-ə-ji), from the Greek *bios*, life (we have already met *biography*, the writing of a life story, in Session 36). In modern practice, scientists do not call themselves plain 'biologists', they specify a particular branch of the study. Thus there is:

microbiology – the study of microscopic forms of life (the derivation is from Greek *micros*, small)

marine biology – the study of all the forms of life in the sea (from Latin *mare*, sea); this is a branch of *oceanography* (see above).

Other important life sciences that do not have *bio-* as part of their name are:

genetics – the study of the workings of biological inheritance (from Greek *genesis*, a beginning, origin); the scientist is a *geneticist* (jə-NET'-i-sist)

ecology – the study of creatures in their natural environment (Greek *oikos*, home: see Session 37)

physiology – the study of the functioning of the body (from Greek *physis*, nature).

The prefix *bio-* also occurs in many other words to show the connection with living things: *biochemistry*, the chemistry of living matter; *biotechnology*, the use of living things (usually bacteria) to power industrial processes; *biodegradable* (adj.), capable of being decomposed by bacteria, etc.

2. The plant kingdom

The two great divisions of life forms are the plant kingdom and the animal kingdom. Plants came first, in evolutionary history. Their study is called *botany* (BOT'-ə-ni), from Greek *botane*, grass for a cow to eat, or by extension any plant; the scientist is a *botanist* (BOT'-ə-nist). Much of botany is of great practical importance in developing new and better crops. One useful branch is *mycology*, the study of fungi (Greek *mykes*, fungus).

3. The animal kingdom

The study of the animal kingdom is known as *zoology*. Be careful of the pronunciation: the two *o*s should be separate, as in *co-operate*, even though there is no hyphen to indicate the separation. Say zōo-OL'-ə-ji (and for the adjective *zoological*, zōō-ə-LOJ'-i-kəl); a *zoo*, a park displaying animals, is short for *zoological gardens*, and is pronounced as one syllable.

The derivation is from Greek *zoion*, an animal. We find the same root in *zodiac*, a diagram used in astrology, which contains the Latin names of a number of animals (*leo*, lion, *taurus*, bull, etc.). It also appears in *spermatozoon*, plural *spermatozoa*, sperm cells (because they used to be thought of as tiny animals in their own right, which they are not).

4. Insects

Flies, bees, beetles, wasps, and other insects are segmented creatures – head, thorax, and abdomen. Where these parts join, there appears to the imaginative eye a 'cutting in' of the body. Hence the branch of zoology dealing with insects is aptly named *entomology* (en'-tə-MOL'-ə-ji), from Greek *en-*, in, plus *tome*, a cutting. The adjective is *entomological* (en'-tə-mə-LOJ'-i-kəl). (Be very careful not to confuse this with *etymology*, your present study, word origins; the derivation is from Greek *etymos*, true, actual.)

The prefix *ec-*, from Greek *ek-*, means *out*. (The Latin prefix, you will recall, is *ex-*.) Combine *ec-* with *tome* to derive the words for surgical procedures in which parts are 'cut out', or removed: *tonsillectomy* (the tonsils), *appendectomy* (the appendix), *mastectomy* (the breast), *hysterectomy* (the uterus), *prostatectomy* (the prostate), etc.

5. Humanity's history

The study of the material remains of the human past is called *archaeology* (ar'-ki-OL'-ə-ji), from the Greek *archaeos*, ancient; so, literally, the study of ancient things. From the same root comes the adjective *archaic*, which is used to mean 'ancient' in a derogatory sense: out-of-date, antiquated. (Do not confuse these with words containing *arch-* meaning chief, as in *patriarch*; these latter have nothing to do with age, however tempting it might be to think so.)

Another root for words concerned with the remote past is *palaeo-*, which is from another Greek adjective meaning 'ancient'. It appears in *palaeontology* (pal'-i-on-TOL'-ə-ji), the study of fossils (from Greek *on, ontos*, a being, a thing that exists; so, literally, the study of things that existed in ancient times). More specifically, we have *palaeobotany*, the study of the plants of prehistoric times, and *palaeoanthropology*, the study of the fossils of early humans (Greek *anthropos*, a human: see Session 25).

Curiously, *palaeography* (pal-i-OG'-rə-fi) does not mean writing about or describing ancient times; it is the study of old handwriting, and not very old at that; an expert in palaeography might be able to tell Henry VIII's writing from Shakespeare's.

Teaser questions for the amateur etymologist – 10

1. Most *satellites* circle in orbit around the Earth. But some are *geostationary* – can you guess what this means, and give its derivation?

2. There is a word derived from the Latin *petra* that literally means 'to turn to stone', but is more usually used to mean 'to frighten thoroughly'. What is it?

3. Can you work out what the science of *palaeoecology* is about?

4. You probably know that a spider is not an insect, and is therefore not an object of study by an entomologist. Construct the word for the science of spiders, using the root *arachno-*, from the Greek *arakhne*, spider.

5. The root *crypto-* comes from Greek *kryptos*, hidden; and from it we get *cryptology*, the science of codes and code-breaking. Can you guess the word for a person who is skilled in writing in code?

(*Answers in Chapter 11*)

Review of etymology

Write in the space provided an English word that uses each prefix, root, or suffix.

1.	*en-*	in	_____
2.	*ek-*	out	_____
3.	*archaeo-*	ancient	_____
4.	*zoo-*	living creature	_____
5.	*-graphy*	writing	_____
6.	*micro-*	small	_____
7.	*physis*	nature	_____
8.	*palaeo-*	ancient	_____
9.	*tome*	cutting	_____
10.	*bios*	life	_____

Can you match the words?

1.	zodiac	a.	the study of fungi
2.	palaeography	b.	the study of word origins
3.	mycology	c.	the science of very small creatures
4.	biotechnology	d.	the study of the body's workings
5.	appendectomy	e.	the science of fossils
6.	microbiology	f.	removal of the appendix
7.	physiology	g.	the study of living things in their environment
8.	palaeontology	h.	an astrological diagram
9.	ecology	i.	the use of bacteria in industry
10.	etymology	j.	the study of old handwriting

Key: 1-h, 2-j, 3-a, 4-i, 5-f, 6-c, 7-d, 8-e, 9-g, 10-b

Do you understand the words?

1.	*Biodegradable* packaging lasts for ever	YES NO
2.	An *entomologist* studies bees and wasps	YES NO
3.	A *spermatozoon* is a kind of animal	YES NO
4.	*Ecology* is the study of financial systems	YES NO
5.	A surgeon will only perform a *mastectomy* as a last resort	YES NO
6.	The 'missing link' is likely to be found by a *palaeoanthropologist*	YES NO
7.	A *botanical* garden is one used for the scientific study of plants	YES NO
8.	If you find dry rot in the house you call in a *mycologist*	YES NO
9.	A *zodiac* is an apparatus used by a *biologist*	YES NO
10.	Routine *tonsillectomy* is an *archaic* procedure	YES NO

Key: 1-N, 2-Y, 3-N, 4-N, 5-Y, 6-Y, 7-Y, 8-Y, 9-N, 10-Y

Baby don't cry

Any word that starts with the root *cryo-* means something to do with freezing (from the Greek *kryos*, frost). Thus *cryogenics* is the branch of physics that deals with very low temperatures, and *cryobiology* is the study of animals and plants that live in sub-zero conditions.

Cryonics is the practice of preserving human bodies frozen in liquid nitrogen, with a view to reviving them at some point in the future when a cure has been found for whatever the person died of.

TEST IV
YOUR FINAL CHECK-UP

Most of this test is about words that you have learnt in Chapters 8, 9, and 10. But there are also 20 questions on words from earlier in the book, to test your overall knowledge.

I Etymology

Root	Meaning	Example
1. *derma*	_____	dermatology
2. *orthos*	_____	orthodontics
3. *psyche*	_____	psychotic
4. *neuron*	_____	neurology
5. *logos*	_____	biology
6. *algos*	_____	neuralgia
7. *agogos*	_____	demagogue
8. *pes, pedis*	_____	pedestrian
9. *paidos (paed–)*	_____	paediatrician
10. *demos*	_____	democracy
11. *oculus*	_____	ocular
12. *iatreia*	_____	psychiatry
13. *metron*	_____	optometrist
14. *geras*	_____	geriatrics
15. *soma*	_____	psychosomatics
16. *pathos*	_____	osteopath
17. *odontos*	_____	orthodontics
18. *pous, podos*	_____	octopus, podium
19. *cheir (chiro–)*	_____	chirography
20. *ophthalmos*	_____	opthalmologist

II   More etymology

1. *graphein*   _____   geography
2. *astron*   _____   astronomy
3. *nautes*   _____   astronaut
4. *ge* (geo-)   _____   geology
5. *zoion*   _____   zoology
6. *calculus*   _____   calculate
7. *oikos*   _____   economics
8. *meteoron*   _____   meteorology
9. *hydor, hydros* _____   hydrology
10. *nomos*   _____   agronomy
11. *petra*   _____   petroleum
12. *bios*   _____   biology
13. *physis*   _____   physiology
14. *tome*   _____   tonsillectomy
15. *sectus*   _____   insect
16. *khoros*   _____   choreography
17. *kardia*   _____   cardiogram
18. *platy*   _____   platypus
19. *therapeia*   _____   psychotherapy
20. *pharmakon*   _____   pharmacist

III   Matching

1. studies volcanoes   a. actuary
2. draws maps   b. astrologer
3. calculates risks   c. entomologist
4. studies drug action   d. cartographer
5. designs buildings   e. cosmologist
6. studies the universe   f. pharmacologist
7. studies word origins   g. etymologist
8. works with X-rays   h. vulcanologist
9. uses a zodiac   i. architect
10. studies insects   j. radiographer

IV   More matching

1. delivers babies   a. paediatrician
2. treats women's ailments   b. cardiologist
3. treats infants and children c. psychiatrist
4. treats skin diseases   d. chiropodist

5. treats skeletal problems
6. is a heart specialist
7. treats mental or emotional
   disturbances
8. treats disorders of the
   nervous system
9. treats minor ailments of
   the feet
10. treats disorders of the blood

e. dermatologist
f. haematologist
g. obstetrician
h. neurologist
i. orthopaedist
j. gynaecologist

V   Recall a word (Chapters 8–10)

1. science of heredity   G _____
2. record of heart action   C _____
3. equally skilful with both the right and left hand   A _____
4. doctor who deals with the problems of ageing   G _____
5. instrument to measure wind speed   A _____
6. beautiful writing   C _____
7. three-legged stand for camera   T _____
8. cancer treatment with chemicals   C _____
9. numerical operations with symbols   A _____
10. person learned in many fields   P _____
11. study of the material nature of stars   A _____
12. belonging to the whole universe   C _____
13. creature with eight feet (or arms)   O _____
14. star-shaped symbol (*)   A _____
15. study of the sea   O _____
16. person who studies earthquakes   S _____
17. expert in the theory of farming   A _____
18. 'sailor among the stars'   A _____
19. technique developed by Sigmund Freud   P _____
20. a speaker's platform   P _____

VI   Recall a word – from earlier chapters

1. mounted branch of the army   C _____
2. literary work following another on the same
   subject   S _____
3. to check whether something is true or correct   V _____
4. looking like a corpse   C _____
5. having two spouses at once   B _____
6. one who starts a fire for revenge   I _____

7. documents to prove a person's standing   C _____
8. killing one's father   P _____
9. to say two different things at once   E _____
10. being skilful with one's hands   D _____
11. pleasure at being alive   J__ D__ V____
12. to identify with someone else's feelings   E _____
13. egg-shaped   O _____
14. person who lives like a hermit   A _____
15. the school or college one attended   A___ M_____
16. fond of being in a jolly crowd   G _____
17. balance of mind, composure   E _____
18. behaving like an uncle   A _____
19. able to speak expressively and persuasively E _____
20. music to play at night   N _____

ANSWERS

Score 1 point for each correct answer.

I Etymology

1- skin, 2-straight, 3-soul, 4-nerve, 5-knowledge, science, 6-pain, 7-leader, 8-foot, 9-child, 10-the people, 11-eye, 12-healing, 13-measurement, 14-old age, 15-body, 16-suffering, 17-tooth, 18-foot, 19-hand, 20-eye
Your score?

II More etymology

1-to write, 2-star, 3-sailor, 4-Earth, 5-living thing, 6-pebble, counter, 7-house, habitat, 8-something in the sky, 9-water, 10-rule, law, 11-rock, stone, 12-life, 13-nature, 14-cut, 15-cut, 16-dance, 17-heart, 18-broad, flat, 19-care, attendance, 20-drug
Your score?

III Matching

1-h, 2-d, 3-a, 4-f, 5-i, 6-e, 7-g, 8-j, 9-b, 10-c
Your score?

IV More matching

1-g, 2-j, 3-a, 4-e, 5-i, 6-b, 7-c, 8-h, 9-d, 10-f
Your score?

V Recall a word (Chapters 8–10)

1- genetics, 2-cardiogram, 3-ambidextrous, 4-geriatrician, 5-anem-
ometer, 6-calligraphy, 7-tripod, 8-chemotherapy, 9-algebra,
10-polymath, 11-astrophysics, 12-cosmic, 13-octopus, 14-asterisk,
15-oceanography, 16-seismologist, 17-agronomist, 18-astronaut,
19-psychoanalysis, 20-podium
Your score?

Recall a word (earlier chapters in the book)

1-cavalry, 2-sequel, 3-verify, 4-cadaverous, 5-bigamy, 6-incendiary,
7-credentials, 8-patricide, 9-equivocate, 10-dexterous, 11-joie de
vivre, 12-empathize, 13-oval or ovoid, 14-ascetic, 15-alma mater,
16-gregarious, 17-equanimity, 18-avuncular, 19-eloquent,
20-nocturne
Your score?

Once again the total possible mark is 100 points. This was the most
difficult test, because of the final section on words that you may have
learnt some weeks ago (and maybe nearly forgotten).

Over 85	Excellent; you can be proud of your improved vocabulary
70–84	Good; it has been well worth your while to study
50–69	Average; you are a better word-user now than when you started, but you should do more revision
26–49	Poor; maybe you should work through the book again
0–25	Unacceptable; you definitely need to start again. Better luck next time!

Invented by . . .

biro – the world-wide ballpoint is called after its inventor, Hungarian Laszlo *Biro* (1899–1985).

tarmac – the durable surface for roads and runways gets its name from *tar* (used to stick it together) plus *macadam*, after John *McAdam*, the Scottish engineer who first used broken-up stones for road-making.

sandwich – the ever-popular 'sarnie' is called after the 4th Earl of *Sandwich*, who wanted something to keep him going during a 24-hour session at the gambling table.

mackintosh – the rubberized waterproof coat is named after its inventor, the Scot Charles *Mackintosh*; note the -k- in the spelling, unlike in the name of the desk-top computer.

diesel – the most widely used engines in the world were invented in 1897 by the German engineer Rudolf *Diesel*, who died in a shipping accident in the Channel.

doily – the little lace mats made the fortune of John *Doily*, a London draper in the eighteenth century.

CHAPTER 11
ARE YOU AN ETYMOLOGIST?

In each of the preceding ten chapters there has been a box with five questions on word derivations. Here are the answers.

CHAPTER 1

1. *Magnanimity* (mag'-nə-NIM'-i-ti). Adjective: *magnanimous* (mag-NAN'-i-məs).

2. *Bilateral* (bī-LAT'-ər-əl), as in a *bilateral* decision, i.e., one made by the two sides or two people involved. On the other hand, a *unilateral* (yōo-ni-LAT'-ər-əl) decision is made by *one* person, without consultation with others.

3. *Transcribe.* Noun: *transcription.* For example, a musical *transcriber* arranges a musical composition for an instrument, group, etc. other than the one for which the work was originally written.

4. *Malaria* was once thought to have been caused by the 'bad air' of swamps; actually, it was (and is) transmitted to humans by infected anopheles mosquitoes breeding and living in swamps and other places where there is stagnant water.

5. *Confection.* The word is hardly used today with this meaning, except perhaps by members of an older generation who remember *confectioner*'s shops.

Check your learning

Prefix, root	Meaning	Example
1. *magnus*	_____	magnanimous
2. *bi-*	_____	bilateral
3. *unus*	_____	unilateral
4. *trans-*	_____	transcribe
5. *malus*	_____	malaria

Key: 1-big, large, great, 2-two, 3-one, 4-across, 5-bad, evil

CHAPTER 2

1. *Circumscription.* To *circumscribe* also means, figuratively, to write (a line) *around (one's freedom of action)*, so that one is restricted or hemmed in, as in 'a life *circumscribed* by poverty'.

2. *Somniloquent* (som-NIL'-ə-kwənt). Noun: *somniloquence* (som-NIL'-ə-kwəns) or *somniloquy* (som-NIL'-ə-kwi), the latter noun also designating the words spoken by the sleeper. One who habitually talks while asleep is a *somniloquist* (som-NIL'-ə-kwist).

3. A *noctambulist* (nok-TAM'-byoo-list) walks at night – *nox, noctis,* night, plus *ambulo,* to walk. Noun: *noctambulism* (nok-TAM'-byoo-liz-əm).

4. *Somnific* (som-NIF'-ik): a *somnific* lecture, film, effect, etc.

5. *Circumambulate* (sər'-kəm-AM'-byoo-layt'). To *circumnavigate* is to sail around – *circum,* around, plus *navis,* ship.

Check your learning

Prefix, root	Meaning	Example
1. *circum-*	_____	circumscribe
2. *somnus*	_____	somniloquent
3. *loquor*	_____	somniloquence
4. *nox, noctis*	_____	noctambulist
5. *ambulo*	_____	circumambulate

Key: 1-around, 2-sleep, 3-to speak, 4-night, 5-to walk

CHAPTER 3

1. To *notify* is, etymologically, to make *known* – *notus* plus *-fy*, a derivation of *facio,* to make.

-Fy, as a verb suffix, means *to make.* So *simplify* is to make simple, *clarify,* to make clear; *liquefy,* to make liquid; *putrefy,* to make (or become) rotten or putrid; *stupefy,* to make stupid, or dumb, with astonishment (note the *-e* preceding the suffix in *liquefy, putrefy, stupefy*); *fortify,* to make strong; *rectify,* to make right or correct; etc., etc.

2. *Chronograph* (KRŌN'-ə-grahf') is an instrument that measures and records short intervals of time.

3. To *generate* is to give birth to, figuratively, or to create or produce, as a turbine *generates* power, a person's presence *generates* fear, etc. The noun is *generation*, which, in another context, also designates the people born and living about the same time.

To *regenerate* is to give birth to again, or to be born again. Some creatures can *regenerate* new limbs or parts if these are lost or cut off – or the limbs or parts *regenerate*.

Re- means, of course, *again*; or, in some words, as *recede*, *regress*, etc., *back*.

4. *Omnipotent* (om-NIP'-ə-tənt) – all-powerful; *omnis* plus *potens*, *potentis*, powerful. *Omnipresent* (om'-ni-PREZ'-ənt) – present all over, or everywhere. Nouns: *omnipotence*, *omnipresence*.

5. *Anaphrodisiac* (ən-af'-rə-DIZ'-i-ak') – both a noun and an adjective. Saltpetre is supposedly an *anaphrodisiac*; so, some people say, is a cold shower, which is highly doubtful.

Check your learning

Prefix, root	Meaning	Example
1. *notus*	_____	notify
2. *chronos*	_____	chronograph
3. *genesis*	_____	generate
4. *omnis*	_____	omnipotent
5. *an-*	_____	anaphrodisiac

Key: 1-known, 2-time, 3-birth, 4-all, 5-not (negative)

CHAPTER 4

1. *Matronymic* (mat'-rə-NIM'-ik). Or, if you prefer to use the Greek root for mother (*meter, metr-*), *metronymic*. The Greek word *metra*, uterus, derives from *meter*, naturally enough, so *metritis* is inflammation of the uterus; *metralgia* is uterine pain; *endometriosis* (en'-dō-mee'-tri-Ō'-sis) is any abnormal condition of the uterine lining – *endo*, inside; *metra*, uterus; *-osis*, abnormal condition.

2. (a) An *incendiary* statement, remark, speech, etc. figuratively sets an audience alight.

(b) *Incense* (IN'-sens) is a substance that sends off a pleasant odour when burnt – often, but not necessarily, to mask unpleasant or telltale smells.

(c) To *incense* (in-SENS') is to anger greatly, i.e., to 'burn up'.

3. (a) *Ardent* (AH'-dənt) – burning with zeal, ambition, love, etc., as an *ardent* suitor, worker, etc.

(b) *Ardour* (AH'-dər) – the noun form of *ardent* – burning passion, zeal, enthusiasm, etc. Alternative noun: *ardency* (AH'-dən-si).

4. *Megaphone*.

5. *Megalopolis* (meg'-ə-LOP'-ə-lis).

Check your learning

Prefix, root	Meaning	Example
1. *onyma*	_____	metronymic
2. *metra*	_____	metritis
3. *ardo*	_____	ardent
4. *megalo*	_____	megalopolis
5. *polis*	_____	police

Key: 1-name, 2-uterus, 3-to burn, 4-big, large, great, 5-city

CHAPTER 5

1. *Vivarium* (vī-VAIR'-i-əm) – enclosed area in which plants and (small) animals live in conditions resembling their natural habitat. The suffix -*ium* usually signifies *place where* – *solarium*, a place for the sun to enter, or where one can sunbathe; *aquarium*, a place for water (Latin *aqua*, water), or fish tank; *podium*, a place for the feet (Greek *pous, podos*, foot), or speaker's platform; *auditorium*, a place for hearing concerts, plays, etc. (Latin *audio*, to hear).

2. (a) *Unicorn* (Latin *cornu*, horn).
   (b) *Uniform*.
   (c) *Unify* (-*fy*, from *facio*, to make)
   (d) *Unity*.
   (e) *Unicycle* (Greek *kyklos*, circle, wheel).

3. *Anniversary* – a year has turned.

4. (a) *Interstate*.
   (b) *International*.
   (c) *Interpersonal*.

5. (a) *Intrastate*.
   (b) *Intranational*.
   (d) *Intramuscular*.

Check your learning

Prefix, root	Meaning	Example
1. *vivo*	_____	survive
2. *cornu*	_____	unicorn
3. *annus*	_____	anniversary
4. *inter*	_____	interstate
5. *intra-*	_____	intrapsychic

Key: 1-to live, 2-horn, 3-year, 4-between, 5-within

CHAPTER 6

1. Women; and you do not have to be a *misogynist* to be afraid of them.

2. *Cynophobe* (SĪ'-nə-fōb). See other phobias in the Appendix.

3. A *gynandromorph* (gīn-AND'-rə-morf) would have the shape of both woman and man at once. Some insects are called this, because they have the sex organs of both sexes. Another word for the same thing is *hermaphrodite* (her-MAF'-rə-dīt), from the names of the Greek god Hermes and goddess Aphrodite.

4. *Monolingual* (mon-o-LING'-wəl).

5. *Philosophy* (fil-OS'-ə-fi) is the love of wisdom: from Greek *philos*, love, plus *sophia*, wisdom.

Check your learning

Prefix, root	Meaning	Example
1. *gyne, gynaikos*	_____	gynophobe
2. *phobos*	_____	cynophobe
3. *aner, andros*	_____	gynandromorph
4. *mono-*	_____	monolingual
5. *sophia*	_____	philosophy

Key: 1-woman, 2-fear, 3-man, 4-single, 5-wisdom

CHAPTER 7

1. *Indolent* (IN'-də-lənt). The noun is *indolence* (IN'-də-ləns). Do not confuse these words with *indigent, indigence*, which mean *poor* and *poverty*, as discussed in Session 29.

2. *Non sequitur* (non SEK'-wi-tə) – 'it does not follow'.

3. (a) *inversion* – prefix *in-* meaning *in, into*, so 'turning inside out' (or upside down).

(b) *subversion* – prefix *sub-* meaning *under, from below*, so 'turning under' (or undermining).

4. *Prehistoric* is *before* history; usually taken as before the invention of writing, which is when history proper can begin.

5. (a) *Superior*
(b) *Supernatural*
(c) *Supervise*

Check your learning

Prefix, root	Meaning	Example
1. *in-*	_____	indolent
2. *sequor*	_____	non sequitur
3. *verto, versus*	_____	subversion
4. *pre-*	_____	prehistory
5. *super-*	_____	superior

Key: 1-not, 2-to follow, 3-to turn, 4-before, 5-over, above

CHAPTER 8

1. *Paedodontics* (pee'-də-DON'-tiks) is the speciality of child dentistry – *paidos*, child, plus *odontos*, tooth. Specialist: *paedodontist*. Adjective: *paedodontic*.

2. *Cardialgia* (kah'-di-AL'-ji-ə), heart pain – *kardia*, heart, plus *algos*, pain.

3. *Odontalgia* (ō'-don-TAL'-ji-ə), toothache.

4. *Carditis* (kah-DĪ'-tis), inflammation of the heart – *kardia*, heart, plus *-itis*, inflammation.

5. *Analgesic* (an-al-JEEZ'-ik) combines negative root *an-* with *algos*, pain.

Check your learning

Prefix, root	Meaning	Example
1. *paidos* (*paed-*)	_____	paedodontics
2. *kardia*	_____	cardialgia
3. *algos*	_____	odontalgia
4. *-itis*	_____	carditis
5. *an-*	_____	analgesic

Key: 1-child, 2-heart, 3-pain, 4-inflammation, 5-not

CHAPTER 9

1. Eighty to eighty-nine years old. From Latin *octoginta*, eighty. People of other ages are as follows:
   (a) 50–59: *quinquagenarian* (kwin'-kwə-ji-NAIR'-i-ən)
   (b) 60–69: *sexagenarian* (seks'-ə-ji-NAIR'-i-ən)
   (c) 70–79: *septuagenarian* (sep'-tyoo-ə-ji-NAIR'-i-ən)
   (d) 90–99: *nonagenarian* (nōn-ə-ji-NAIR'-i-ən)

2. *Metronome* is derived from Greek *metron*, measurement, and *nomos*, rule or law. Literally, therefore, 'rule by measurement', it is a machine (nowadays usually electronic) that emits a regular beat to help the musician to keep time.

3. *Chiromancy* is the art of predicting the future by reading the hand (Greek *chiro-*, hand).

4. *Telepathy* (tə-LEP'-ə-thi), from Greek *tele-*, far, at a distance. The adjective is *telepathic* (tel-ə-PATH'-ik).

5. *Psychometrics* is the science of measuring aspects of the personality with tests, questionnaires, and so forth. It is derived from Greek *psyche*, soul, plus *metron*, measurement. The practitioner is either a *psychometrician* (sī'-kə-met-RISH'-ən) or a *psychometrist* (sī-KOM'-ə-trist).

Check your learning

Prefix, root	Meaning	Example
1. *octoginta*	_____	octogenarian
2. *nomos*	_____	metronome
3. *-mancy*	_____	chiromancy
4. *tele-*	_____	telepathic
5. *metron*	_____	psychometrics

Key: 1-eighty, 2-rule, law 3-prediction, 4-far, at a distance, 5-measurement

CHAPTER 10

1. A *geostationary* (jee-ō-STAY'-shən-ə-ri) satellite is one that stays in the same place above the Earth all the time (because it is orbiting at exactly the same speed as the Earth rotates). The derivation is from Greek *ge-*, Earth, plus Latin *statio*, standing still (note hybrid derivation).

2. *Petrify* (PET'-rə-fī), combining Latin *petra*, rock or stone, with *-fy*, from *facio*, to make, turn into.

3. The study of the interrelationships of living creatures in prehistoric times; from *palaeo-*, ancient, plus *ecology*, which you already know about.

4. *Arachnology* (a-rək-NOL'-ə-ji).

5. *Cryptographer* (krip-TOG'-rə-fə).

Check your learning

Prefix, root	Meaning	Example
1. *geo-*	_____	geostationary
2. *petra*	_____	petrify
3. *palaeo-*	_____	palaeoecology
4. *arachnos*	_____	arachnology
5. *crypto-*	_____	cryptographer

Key: 1-Earth, 2-rock, stone, 3-ancient, 4-spider, 5-hidden

Animals from far-away places

Some exotic animals that were known to the Greeks and Romans have 'European' names: thus *hippopotamus*, literally 'horse of the river' (Greek *hippos*, horse, and *potamos*, river) and *rhinoceros*, literally, 'horned nose' (Greek *rhis, rhinos*, nostril, hence nose, plus *keros*, horned).

Later on, explorers brought back not just the animals themselves (usually dead) but also reports of what their names were in their native habitat.

Moose, opossum, and *skunk* are all the original names of these creatures in Algonquian, an American Indian language.

Panda is from Nepalese.

The languages of the Congo basin in Africa have given us *chimpanzee* and *okapi*, the giraffe-like animal not discovered by Europeans until 1900.

Zebra is not an African name (though it looks as if it should be); it is from Italian. But a *gnu* is purely African: the word is straight from the Xhosa language, which includes many clicking noises that Europeans find hard to say.

CHAPTER 12
HOW TO KEEP BUILDING YOUR VOCABULARY

STEP ONE. *You must become actively receptive to new words.*

Words won't come chasing after you – you must train yourself to be on a constant lookout, in your reading and listening, for any words that other people know and you don't.

STEP TWO. *You must read more.*

STEP THREE. *You must learn to add to your own vocabulary the new words you meet in your reading.*

When you see an unfamiliar word, do not skip over it impatiently. Instead, pause for a moment and say it over to yourself – get used to its sound and appearance. Then puzzle out its possible meaning in the context of the sentence.

STEP FOUR. *You must open your mind to new ideas.*

Think for a few minutes of the areas of human knowledge that may possibly be unknown to you – psychology, semantics, science, art, music, or whatever. Then attack one of these areas methodically – by reading books in the field.

STEP FIVE. *You must set a goal.*

If you do nothing about your vocabulary, you will learn, at most, twenty-five to fifty new words in the next twelve months. *By conscious effort you can learn several thousand.* Set yourself a goal of finding several new words *every day*.

Vocabulary building *snowballs*. The results of each new day's search will be greater and greater.

Enjoy the quest!

It's a battlefield

A *bayonet*, the pointed blade that is fixed on to the end of a rifle barrel, gets its name from the city of *Bayonne*, in south-west France.

The *dum-dum* bullet has a soft case that expands when it hits flesh and therefore causes much worse injuries than ordinary bullets. Credit for this nasty invention goes to the town of *Dum-dum*, in India.

The colour *magenta*, a rich purplish-red, takes its name from the town of Magenta in Italy, because of the blood shed at a battle there.

The name of a *marathon* race comes from a great moment in ancient Greek history. The Athenians had unexpectedly defeated the huge Persian army at the village of *Marathon*, and one man ran all the way to Athens to bring news of the victory to the city. The distance was 26 miles.

Pencil it in

When you meet a new word in the course of your daily reading, underline it with a *mental* pencil. That is, pause for a second and attempt to figure out its meaning from its use in the sentence or from its etymological root or prefix, if it contains one you have studied. Make a mental note of it, say it aloud once or twice – and then go on reading.

A French headache

You know, of course, that a *boudoir* is a lady's private dressing room. But did you know what the literal meaning is? It is 'a place to sulk in' – from the French *bouder*, to sulk.

Go on, -geon

How many words can you think of that end in *-geon*?
   Here are two to start you off:
   bludgeon – to batter someone, or the stick you do this with
   curmudgeon – a sulky, bad-tempered person

APPENDIX
What Are You Afraid Of?
— some esoteric phobias

You will recognize many of the Greek roots on which these words are constructed.

air: aerophobia
animals: zoophobia
beauty: callophobia
blood: haematophobia
breasts: mastophobia
burglars: scelerophobia
burial alive: taphephobia
cats: ailurophobia
change: neophobia
children: paedophobia
colours: chromophobia
crowds: ochlophobia
darkness: nyctophobia
death: thanatophobia
depths: bathophobia
disease: pathophobia
doctors: iatrophobia
dogs: cynophobia
dying: thanatophobia
emptiness: kenophobia
everything: pantophobia
eyes: ophthalmophobia
faeces: coprophobia

fear: phobophobia
feet: podophobia
fire: pyrophobia
fish: ichthyophobia
fog: homichlophobia
food: cibophobia
foreigners: xenophobia
frogs: batrachophobia
ghosts: phantasmophobia
hands: chirophobia
hair: trichophobia
healers or healing:
  iatrophobia
heat: thermophobia
hell: stygiophobia
homosexuality: homophobia*
horses: hippophobia
insects: entomophobia
knives: aichmophobia
knowledge: gnosiophobia
large things: megalophobia
light: photophobia
lightning: astrophobia

---

* This is a horrid word as well as a horrid thing: as it stands, it only means *fear of the same*.

males: androphobia
many things: polyphobia
marriage: gamophobia
medicine: pharmacophobia
mice: musophobia
mirrors: spectrophobia
motherhood: metrophobia
motion: kinesophobia
nakedness: gymnophobia
needles: belonophobia
night: nyctophobia
odours: osmophobia
old age: geraphobia
old men: gerontophobia
pain: algophobia
people: demophobia
plants: botanophobia
pleasure: hedonophobia
poison: toxicophobia
poverty: peniophobia
prostitutes: pornophobia
punishment: poinophobia
rain: ombrophobia
red: erythrophobia
rivers: potamophobia
sea: thalassophobia
sex: genophobia
sexual intercourse: coitophobia
skin: dermatophobia
sleep: hypnophobia
small things: microphobia
smothering: pnigerophobia
snakes: ophidiophobia
snow: chionophobia
solitude: autophobia; monophobia

sounds: acousticophobia
speaking: lalophobia
speech: logophobia
spiders: arachnophobia
stairs: climacophobia
stars: siderophobia
stealing: kleptophobia
stillness: eremiophobia
strangers: xenophobia
strength: sthenophobia
study: logophobia
sunlight: heliophobia
tapeworms: taeniophobia
taste: geumophobia
technology: technophobia
teeth: odontophobia
thieves: kleptophobia
thinking: phronemophobia
thirst: dipsophobia
thunder: brontophobia
time: chronophobia
togetherness: synophobia
travel: hodophobia
ugliness: cacophobia
voices: phemophobia
vomiting: emetophobia
walking: basiphobia
watching: scoptophobia
water: hydrophobia
weakness: asthenophobia
wealth: plutophobia
wind: anemophobia
women: gynophobia
words: logophobia
work: ergophobia